KIDS, DRUGS & THE LAW

About the author:

Attorney David G. Evans has worked in the chemical dependency field for over a decade. He serves as Chairman of the Alcoholism and Drug Law Reform Committee of the American Bar Association, which was responsible for the ABA Commission on Youth Alcohol and Drug Problems. Mr. Evans is a member of the National Organization on Legal Problems of Education and the National Association of Alcoholism and Drug Abuse Counselors. He has lectured extensively on legal aspects of chemical dependency in adults and children and has authored numerous articles. He is the author of *A Practitioner's Guide to Alcoholism and the Law* published by Hazelden and of a Hazelden audio tape entitled *Confidentiality and the Law.*

About the book:

Can a minor consent to chemical dependency treatment? Are parents liable for their children's criminal or civil misdeeds? Can teachers be sued for trying to help a student with alcohol and other drug problems? This book answers these and many other questions concerning children, parents, school officials, and treatment providers and shows how they are affected by laws concerning alcohol and other drug use and treatment.

KIDS, DRUGS & THE LAW

David G. Evans, Esq.

First published June, 1985.

ISBN: 0-89486-283-9

Printed in the United States of America.

Editor's Note:
    Hazelden Educational Materials offers a variety of informa-
tion on chemical dependency and related areas. Our publica-
tions do not necessarily represent Hazelden or its programs,
nor do they officially speak for any Twelve Step organization.

DEDICATION

To Katie.

To my parents, who had to contend with my illness and whose love and support made the difference between life and death.

To Mrs. Geraldine O. Delaney and the staff of Alina Lodge for giving me a standard to recover by.

To John C. Shepherd, Esq., President of the American Bar Association, for his leadership in establishing the ABA Advisory Commission on Youth Alcohol and Drug Problems.

To those young people who are recovering, or need to.

PREFACE

My daughter Katie is a year old, and I have a lot to learn as a parent. I don't know how Katie will deal with alcohol and other drugs. My wife and I will set a positive example, and we will help Katie understand the risks of drug use. We also have a responsibility to help society move towards positive solutions. We hope the world will be a better place when Katie is a teenager.

A sum from the royalties of this book will be used to establish a fund to provide treatment for young people at a chemical dependency rehabilitation center.*

Many people have helped with this book. In particular, I want to thank William J. Kane, J.D., CAC, a consultant to the National Council on Alcoholism of North Jersey, and Gail Gleason Milgram, Ed.D., Professor/Director of Education, Rutgers Center of Alcohol Studies, for their very detailed comments and proofreading.

I also wish to express my gratitude to Abigail J. Healy, Liaison for Alcohol Issues at the White House; Diane Grieder of New Beginnings-Serenity Lodge, Chesapeake, Virginia; John J. Ryan, J.D., CAC, Business Administrator, Alina Lodge, Blairstown, New Jersey; Tom Griffin, Manager of Hazelden-Cork Sports Education and Health Promotion

---

*Chemical dependency is an addiction to mood-altering drugs, including alcohol.

Services, Minneapolis, Minnesota and the other Hazelden staff who commented on the book; Carolyn Burns, National Federation of Parents for Drug-Free Youth, Silver Spring, Maryland; William M. Burns, President, Straight Talk Productions, Silver Spring, Maryland; Brian Connelly of KIDS of Bergen County, New Jersey; and my pigeon with the Harvard J.D., M.B.A. who wishes to remain anonymous; and others who provided comments or otherwise helped. I also want to thank my cousin Alice M. Evans, M.A., for her editorial and creative assistance.

My love and gratitude to my wife, Toos, who went through a pregnancy, childbirth, and the first experiences of motherhood as this book was being written. I thank her for her patience with me when I worked on the book instead of helping her with diapers and other duties.

The Author
Lawrenceville, New Jersey 1985

The opinions expressed in this book are solely those of the author. The publisher does not represent itself as an authority on law. This book is for general informational purposes only. The users of this book should consult their own attorney for specific legal advice.

CONTENTS

Chapter

INTRODUCTION

This book is for parents, teachers, school officials, treatment providers, attorneys, and anyone concerned about alcohol and other drug problems of young people. Our knowledge of how to assist parents, schools, and government to help these young people is in its infancy. Our knowledge of the legal aspects of this area is almost nonexistent. This book is a first step in filling this void. It will discuss major legal issues that occur when children use or misuse alcohol and other drugs. This book will answer many questions and raise a few. My intent is to inform you so you can use the law as a tool for recovery. If the law in your state or on the federal level is not helpful, this book will make you aware of the legal issues involved so you can work for law reform.

The first chapters are a discussion of the basic legal rights and responsibilities of families, parents, schools, and government in relation to children. The next chapters, on treatment issues and confidentiality, will discuss how to help children into treatment and the rights of children, parents, schools, and treatment providers. Finally, we will discuss the legal aspects of children of alcoholics and other drug addicts. At the end of the book, there are additional materials on how to do legal research.

When the book refers to "young people" or "children," it means those people who are below the age of majority, or the legal drinking age, as the case may be. These ages will vary under state law. When this book refers to "drugs," alcohol is being included as a drug.

This book refers to state and federal laws, and although this book answers many questions, laws change or are sometimes in conflict with other laws. If you are unsure about a legal situation, get legal advice to ensure your actions are in compliance with current law. Your attorney will find this book very helpful in advising you. Why should you read this book if it suggests that you consult an attorney anyway? Well, you or your attorney may not be aware there is a problem that needs attention. This book will tell you where the problems are *and* how to find the solutions.

Many people feel anxiety about legal issues. People are often afraid to do something because they may be sued. Many think they have no power when dealing with the law. Don't worry! The law is on your side in helping children with chemical dependency problems.

I
THE RIGHTS AND RESPONSIBILITIES
OF FAMILIES

We all have mothers, fathers, and maybe brothers, sisters, and other relatives or guardians. A family is a legal entity, as well as a group of people. This chapter and the next will discuss families as legal entities and will look at their general legal rights and responsibilities. In later chapters we will look at the rights and responsibilities of schools and government and deal with specific issues concerning alcohol and other drug treatment for children and their parents.

Legal Rights of Families

The law recognizes a "private realm of family life" that is afforded legal protection.[1] In fact, freedom of personal choice in matters of family life is one of the liberties protected by the U.S. Constitution.[2] The usual understanding of the term *family* implies biological relationships; however, the law also recognizes that psychological families may exist beyond a blood relationship, as in the case of a foster parent. The U.S. Supreme Court has stated the importance of families stems from "the intimacy of daily association, and from the role it plays in promoting a way of life" through the care and instruction of children.[3] In the United States, we want people to have their natural family rights protected. We want people and their families to grow with their own beliefs and customs, thus protecting the democracy and diversity of our nation. But family members cannot do as they wish all of the time. Families have responsibilities which largely involve children.

3

General Family Responsibilities toward Children

The law views a family as a self-governing entity under the control of the parents.[4] The parents have the responsibility not to be evil, neglectful of a child, or inflict unreasonable punishment. Parents must also support their children as best they can according to their means and circumstances and must provide the "necessaries" for proper care of children, which include shelter, food, clothing, education, and medical attention.[5] This applies whether the parents are married or not.

Parental Rights

Parents have the right to control, restrain, and discipline a child and the right to control the child's education.[6] Parents also have the right to make decisions regarding the medical care of their children. Parental consent must generally be secured before any medical treatment is begun which might entail danger to the life or health of the child, or keep the child from being in the parents' custody. In treatment situations, the will of the parents controls except when there is an emergency or parental neglect, or when the law gives the child the right to consent to treatment on his or her own.[7] The chapter on treatment will discuss this further.

Parents also have rights to custody, companionship, earnings, and services of their children.[8] Parents may be able to sue someone who deprives them of these rights if that person does so by injuring the child, harboring the child, or by direct enticement or abduction of the child, or through other actions.[9]

Removal of Parental Rights

Under certain circumstances, if there is abuse or neglect of a child, the state can intervene and remove the child from parental custody or otherwise curtail parental rights. Parental

4

rights can also be terminated by the *emancipation* of a child.[10] Emancipation occurs when a child can make some or all decisions regarding his or her medical care, education, or livelihood. Emancipation can occur when the child reaches the age of majority, or when parents agree that a child is able to take care of him- or herself, leave home, and earn a living. Sometimes this occurs when parents unilaterally give up parental rights and the child assumes his or her own care.[11] If a minor marries or enlists in the military, emancipation also occurs. Parental rights can also be curtailed when one parent is given sole legal custody of a child.

When parents are divorced, or were never married, the parent who has legal custody of the child has greater legal power to make decisions regarding the child. The noncustodial parent loses some parental rights and may only have to be consulted regarding the child's welfare.

In Loco Parentis

Someone can stand *in loco parentis* (in the place of the parent)[12] when a person or institution has assumed the obligations of parents without a formal, legal adoption. People *in loco parentis* can be held liable for failure to perform duties imposed on them by this situation. *In loco parentis* usually arises when the parents consent to it, and a person or institution makes it clear that there is an assumption of a parental role. It is a temporary condition and may be ended at will by the surrogate parent or by the child.[13] Generally, *in loco parentis* can apply when a child is in school, a residential institution such as a boarding school, a foster home, or with stepparents, grandparents, or other relatives who have assumed parental roles.[14]

Guardianship of a Child

A guardian is a person appointed by a court, or through other legal means such as a will, to be legally responsible for

5

a child unable to care for him- or herself. A *ward* is the child who is cared for by the guardian.[15] There are many types of guardianship, depending on how much power the court or will gives the guardian. These can include guardianship over the estate, property, and custody of a child, or a *guardian ad litem* who is a person who manages a lawsuit for a child. Very often attorneys are appointed by a court to be *guardian ad litem* and to represent a child's legal interests.[16]

In light of the above, when the term *parent* is used in this book, it can include anyone who is a biological or adoptive parent, a legally appointed guardian, or someone *in loco parentis*. Consult your state law to determine how parental rights are established in your state.

Children's Family Rights

Children have a right to care and support that meets the minimum accepted community standard.[17] This is more than just food, clothing, and shelter, and may include direct, continuous, and intimate care by adults committed to this responsibility.[18] Children have the right to be nurtured and to have reasonable opportunities for development.[19] Parents who exceed the bounds of reasonable discipline, who abuse a child, or ignore medical treatment for a child do not provide this basic standard of care.[20]

Chapter 1
ENDNOTES

1. Prince v. Massachusetts, 321 U.S. 158, 166 (1944); see also Smith v. Organization of Foster Families, 431 U.S. 816 (1977).
2. Cleveland Board of Education v. La Fleur, 414 U.S. 632, 639, 640 (1974).
3. Wisconsin v. Yoder, 406 U.S. 205, 231-233 (1972).
4. *American Jurisprudence,* 2nd ed. (Rochester, NY: The Lawyers' Cooperative Publishing Co., San Francisco,

   CA: Bancroft Whitney Co., 1971) 59, Parent and Child,
   sec. 8.
5. Ibid., sec. 54.
6. Ibid., sec. 24.
7. Ibid., sec. 15.
8. Ibid., sec. 106; and Inge N. Dobelis, ed., *Reader's
   Digest Family Legal Guide* (Pleasantville, NY, 1981),
   p.707.
9. *American Jurisprudence,* 59, Parent and Child, sec. 107-
   10; Friedrichsen v. Niemotka, 71 NJS 399, 400 (1962).
10. *American Jurisprudence,* 59, Parent and Child, sec. 93.
11. Ibid., sec. 93-5.
12. Ibid., sec. 88.
13. Ibid., sec. 89.
14. Ibid., sec. 89-92.
15. *Reader's Digest Family Legal Guide,* pp. 512-514; and
    NJSA 3A:6-16 (10) (c), NJSA 3A:6-36, NJ RULE 4:83.
16. *Reader's Digest Family Legal Guide,* pp. 512-514.
17. Gerald T. Hannah, Walter P. Christian, and Hewitt B.
    Clark, *Preservation of Client Rights* (New York: The
    Free Press, 1981) p. 45.
18. Ibid.
19. Ibid.
20. Ibid.

II
LIABILITY OF PARENTS, OTHER ADULTS, AND CHILDREN

Are parents liable for their children's actions? Can parents be sued if they allow their children to drink and drive? Who is liable for acts of vandalism committed by children under the influence of alcohol or other drugs? Can parents sue other adults who provided alcohol or other drugs to their children? This chapter will address these and related issues.

Liability of Parents

Parents are not always responsible for the torts of their children. A *tort* is a private or civil wrong, or injury resulting from the breach of a legal duty.[1] For example, if you fail to drive carefully and injure another, you have committed a tort. We all have a legal duty not to hurt others through negligence or malice.

If a parent is in no way connected to a child's tort, there may be no liability unless the tort is in the category of being willful, malicious, or violent and destructive, i.e., the child is not just negligent, but purposefully sets out to cause damage, or knows that the action has a high probability of damage.[2] This principle does not apply where a court has taken the child from the parents and has placed the child in a prison or other detaining facility. In these cases, the parents are not liable when the child commits a tort in such a facility.[3] Generally, though, if the tort is of the willful, malicious, or destructive variety, the parents may be directly liable even if they had nothing to do with it. Most states, however, limit the liability of parents in these cases to a certain dollar amount such as $500 or $2,500. Check your state law on this.[4]

There may be another situation where parents are liable, even if they are not at fault. This rule applies when children are of "tender years," i.e., too young to be considered capable of making any decision. For example, one case held the parents responsible when their six-year-old child ran into a person with his bike.[5] Except for situations like this, parents are not usually liable for negligent acts of their children. However, if the parents are negligent in some way, or otherwise contribute to the acts of their children, the parents can be held liable, and there is no set financial limit of liability. This may apply even if the child's acts are not malicious or violent.[6]

Parents can be liable if a child acts on behalf of a parent as an agent, servant, or as an employee.[7] They may also be liable if they know the child is committing a tort and make no effort to restrain the child. Such a parent is considered to have authorized or consented to the act.[8] Parents may also be liable if they provide the child with a dangerous instrument such as a gun, which because of the child's inexperience or immaturity, may become a source of danger to others.[9] Parental liability can also occur if they fail to control a child when they knew, or should have known, that injury to another was a probable consequence.[10] Parents may be at fault if they have knowledge of a wrongdoing and consent to it, direct it, sanction it, or if they approve or participate in it.[11] These rules also apply to criminal acts. When a parent directs a child to commit a criminal act or consents to it, the parent may also be guilty of a crime. For example, if a parent allows a child to violate a curfew ordinance, it has been held constitutional to punish the parent.[12]

What do these rules mean for parents of children who abuse alcohol and other drugs? Are parents liable for *any* acts that these children do under the influence of drugs? First of all, parents may not be under a duty to absolutely prevent a child from using drugs.[13] Parents are only liable if they are negligent, condone a child's actions, or if the child's actions are willfully malicious. What are some examples of this? If parents allow a child to drive their car, under the "family car doctrine" parents can be held liable for what the child does with the car. If the child gets drunk or uses other drugs, the parents may be liable for any damage resulting from an accident.[14] If your state has laws prohibiting adults from giving or selling alcohol or other drugs to minors and you do so, you may be both criminally and civilly liable. For example, the city of Glen Ellyn, Illinois, passed a law making it a crime for adults to allow minors who are not their own children to drink on premises owned by those adults.[15] In Glen Ellyn, if there is a beer party occurring on such premises, the adults are subject to arrest and a fine of up to $500, and they may be liable for the torts of the children who were on their premises.

Social Hosts

A parent or other adult "social host" who gives a child alcohol and knows the child may drive, may be liable for any automobile accidents that occur as a result of the child's drinking and driving.[16] Parents who provide beer for children's parties should be aware that this is an illegal and dangerous action, especially if the children will drive afterwards. This principle may also apply if the parents have knowledge that the children may be drinking at a party in the home, even if the parents did not supply the alcohol or are not present. For example, if the parents walked in on a party and saw drinking or knew through other means that alcohol was present, they might be liable if they did not take corrective action. They should call the other parents or the police and get the children properly escorted home so that no one drives while impaired. This may make the parents unpopular with the kids, but it's

11

better than getting their life savings cleaned out in a lawsuit.

If a parent knows a child is selling drugs at home to other children and does not stop it, the parents may be liable to suit by other parents for damages.[17]

Drinking at Home or Elsewhere

Some states allow minor children to drink at home and/or as part of a religious ceremony. Although this may be legal, parents may be liable if they allowed the children, after drinking, to drive or to take other actions that might cause damage.

In those states where kids are not allowed to drink at all some parents argue that they will drink somewhere else, which may be more dangerous. Parents who are concerned about this should ask themselves why their kids are drinking at all, if such drinking is illegal and unsafe. These parents may feel that illegal or not, kids will drink, and it is better to allow drinking at home, or to prepare for it if it occurs outside the home. One parent I know keeps a $50 bill by the front door of his home for cab fare in case his daughter needs a ride home. If she uses the money, there are no questions asked.

Another method for getting kids back home safely is to organize a program using volunteers to provide rides to kids who call in to a central office. The rides are provided for kids who are drunk or who don't want to ride with someone who has been drinking. Confidentiality is protected. Some parents oppose the concept because they feel it supports underage drinking by implying that it is all right for kids to drink as much as they want because someone will take care of them. They also argue that there is no sense in having a drinking age of 21 unless society enforces and supports it.

Liability of Other Adults

Many states have "dramshop" laws or "civil damage acts." These laws make people who sell or give alcoholic beverages to intoxicated persons (including minors) liable for any damages to third parties injured by the intoxicated person.[18] The most common lawsuit involves a situation where a patron leaves a bar and gets into a drunk driving accident. In order to prove such a case, the injured party usually must show that the gift or sale of alcohol was a cause of the person's intoxication (although it does not have to be the sole cause) and that the intoxication was a cooperating, concurring, or directly contributing cause of the damage.[19] It is logical to assume that such laws will apply to other drug intoxication also.

Dramshop laws can be very effective in preventing alcohol sales to minors because financial damages awarded to victims are often substantial. Dramshop laws have been endorsed by the 1983 Presidential Commission on Drunk Driving and the National Highway Traffic Safety Administration, among others.[20]

Sale of Drug Paraphernalia

Most states outlaw the sale of drug paraphernalia.[21] This may include the sale of any equipment, products, and materials of any kind which are used or intended to be used with any illegal drug. Although some of these laws have been attacked on constitutional grounds, they have held up if worded properly.[22] Parents concerned about sales of drug paraphernalia in their state should consult their local prosecutor's office for advice on their state law. If you have no state law prohibiting such sales, the Federal Drug Enforcement Administration in Washington can advise you on how to get a good model law passed in your state.[23]

Interfering with Parental Relationships

A person who unlawfully takes or withholds a child from the legal custody of a parent is committing a tort and/or a crime. So, too, anyone who unlawfully entices away or harbors a child may be committing a tort or a crime.[24] This may not apply when a person only seeks to emotionally alienate parent and child. It applies where there is an active effort to take the child from lawful parental custody. The enticing and harboring must be willful and with knowledge that the parents' rights are being violated. This may not apply when a child runs away and someone harbors the child temporarily to protect it.[25] However, if someone entices a child with alcohol or other drugs and tries to deprive the parents of the child's custody, the parents may have a right to sue, as well as file criminal charges.

Treatment programs in states where minors have rights to treatment should not fear that they will be sued for depriving parents of a child's custody. In states where the child has no rights to treatment, the programs should obtain a court order to allow them to provide treatment if they wish to do so over the parents' objections (see Chapter 5 on Treatment).

What about situations where parents exercise "tough love" and ask a child to leave the family home? Tough love can be exercised when parents give a child the choice of going into a recovery program or leaving home. If the child decides to leave, can the parents sue other adults who provide shelter for the child? First of all, by asking the child to leave, the parents may have emancipated the child and waived some or all of their parental rights. Secondly, they cannot say another party has enticed the child away when they were the ones who asked the child to leave. This certainly applies if the child is an adult. One parent, who asked a drug-abusing eighteen-year-old to leave home, wanted to go to court to get the child to stop living with a drug-abusing friend. The parent had no recourse except to try to get the child committed under the adult mental health commitment law. These risks may be worth it to those parents who have no other choice. Parents contemplating such actions should only do so with professional advice from an experienced chemical dependency counselor.

Liability of Minors to Pay for Damages

In general, minors can be held personally liable for injuries they cause others. For example, in some states, minors have had to pay monetary damages for assault and battery, trespassing, seduction of another minor, fraud, and negligence. However, sometimes the degree of mental intent needed to prove the above cases is difficult to ascertain because of the minor's immaturity. In addition, most minors don't have any money, so it's not profitable to sue them.

Lawsuits by Children against Parents and Vice Versa

Generally, the law does not allow minor children to sue parents or parents to sue minor children. This rule may not apply where the child is emancipated, or where the actions of a parent are malicious, wanton, or willful in character.[26] These cases are very rare, and the courts appear to frown on them.[27]

Avoiding Liability Problems

Don't allow your children or other children to unlawfully use, sell, or give away alcohol or other drugs on your premises. You should not allow your child or another child to drive your car if you have any knowledge they will use drugs. It's hard to do this alone. You will need help from other parents, schools, police, and professionals.

Even if your child does drink or use other drugs, you will be better off if you are able to discuss it with your child. An open dialogue will allow you to take corrective measures. There are many books on how to deal with these issues.[28] Your child's life may depend on your knowledge in this area, so take the time to read and get help. Many parents have found it helpful to join a parents' support group. There are many available.[29]

Chapter 2
ENDNOTES

1. Steven H. Gifis, *Law Dictionary,* (Woodbury, NY: Barron's Educational Series, Inc., 1975), p. 210.
2. Arnold O. Ginnow and George Gordon, eds., *Corpus Juris Secundum,* (St. Paul, MN: West Publishing Company), 67A, Parent and Child VI Tort Liability and Rights of Action, sec. 123.
3. Ibid.
4. Inge N. Dobelis, ed., *Reader's Digest Family Legal Guide,* (Pleasantville, NY, 1981), pp. 1092-3 (these pages have charts on state laws regarding parental liability).
5. Turner v. Bucher, 308 So 2d 270.
6. *American Jurisprudence,* 2nd ed. (Rochester, NY: The Lawyers' Cooperative Publishing Co., San Francisco, CA: Bancroft-Whitney Co., 1971) 59, Parent and Child IV Liability for Acts of Child, sec. 130.
7. Ginnow and Gordon, *Corpus Juris Secundum,* 67 A, Parents and Child, sec. 124.
8. Ibid.
9. *American Jurisprudence,* 59, Parent and Child, sec. 131, 132.
10. Ibid., sec. 133.
11. Ibid., sec. 136.
12. Eastlake v. Ruggiero, 220 NE 2d 126.
13. Moore v. Crumpton, 285 SE 2d 842.
14. *Reader's Digest Family Legal Guide,* p. 469. See pp. 1164-5 for chart of state laws.
15. Village of Glen Ellyn, Illinois, Ordinance #2767-VC.
16. Cartwright v. Hyatt Corp., 460 F Supp 80 (D.D.C. 1978), and Linn v. Rand, 140 N.J. Super 212 (App. Div. 1976); see Kelly v. Gwinnell, 96 NJ 538 (1984) for social host liability; see Davis v. Sam Goody, 195 N.J.S. 423 (1984) for corporate host liability; also Fla. Rev. stat. 5.768.125 (1983), 53 A.L.R. 3rd 1285, 1286 (1973).

17. Hugler v. Rose, 451 N.Y.S. 2nd 478 (1982), and Comeau v. Lulas, 455 N.Y.S. 2nd 871 (1982).
18. *American Jurisprudence,* 45, Intoxicating Liquors, sec. 554; and see The Model Alcoholic Beverage Retail Licensee Liability Act of 1985, a preliminary draft, Prevention Research Group, Medical Research Institute of San Francisco, 2532 Durant Ave., Berkeley, CA 94704.
19. *American Jurisprudence,* 45, Intoxicating Liquors, sec. 582.
20. *Presidential Commission on Drunk Driving* (Washington, D.C.) U.S. Government Printing Office 1983-427-056-814/233, p.11; and see 48 Fed. Reg. 5545 (1985).
21. 58 *Notre Dame Law Review* 833,842,3 (1983).
22. Hoffman Estates v. Flipside, 455 U.S. 489 (1982) and Florida Businessmen for Free Enterprise v. City of Hollywood, 673 F 2nd 1213 (1982).
23. Model Drug Paraphernalia Act, Drug Enforcement Administration, U.S. Department of Justice, Washington, D.C. (1979).
24. Ginnow and Gordon, *Corpus Juris Secundum* 67 A, Parent and Child, sec. 130.
25. Ibid., sec. 131.
26. Ibid., sec. 127-9.
27. *American Jurisprudence,* 59 Parent and Child, sec. 148.
28. Gail G. Milgram, *What, When and How to Talk to Children About Alcohol and Other Drugs: A Guide for Parents,* (Center City, MN: Hazelden, 1983). (Other Hazelden books and pamphlets can be obtained from the Hazelden catalog. For a copy call toll free (800) 328-9000, Order No. 1078A); John E. Donovan and R. Jessor, "Adolescent Problem Drinking," *Journal of Studies in Alcohol,* 39 (1978); B. F. Dykeman, "Teenage Alcoholism — Detecting Those Early Warning Signals," *Adolescence,* Vol. 14, (Summer 1979) pp. 251-4; Joan K. Jackson, "The Adjustment of the Family to the Crisis of

Alcoholism," *Quarterly Journal of Studies of Alcohol* 15:4, (December 1974) pp. 562-586; E. M. Jellenik, *The Disease Concept of Alcoholism,* (New Haven: Hillhouse Press, 1960); H. Kaplan and A. Pokorny, "Self-Attitudes and Alcohol Use Among Adolescents," in F. A. Seixas, *Currents in Alcoholism,* Vol. 2, 1974; C. Steiner, *Games Alcoholics Play* (New York: Ballantine Books, 1971); Marsha Manatt, Ph.D., *Parents, Peers and Pot II,* (Rockville, MD: National Institute on Drug Abuse, 1983).

29.　For a family group in your area, contact the National Federation of Parents for Drug Free Youth, 1820 Franwall Ave., Suite 16, Silver Spring, MD 20902; and contact the Al-Anon Family Groups, One Park Ave., New York, NY 10016, for alcohol problems; for other drug problems, contact Nar-Anon, P.O. Box 2562, Palos Verdes Peninsula, CA 90274. Also, you can call your local alcohol or other drug abuse agency for help.

III
GOVERNMENT

Although our society protects the independence of families, sometimes government steps in when families don't function, don't exist, or when family members break the law or are ill. The government, whether it is federal, state, or local, has this power under the doctrine of *parens patriae,* which in Latin means "parent of the country." *Parens patriae* is the government's sovereign power of guardianship over citizens who are unable to act or care for themselves.[1] This power is based on the government's duty to protect people, and on its interest in the perpetuation of a just and stable society.[2]

State Power over Children and Families

The state has the power to protect children from their parents and other adults, to compel children to obey parental authority, and to require children to attend school.[3] The state can also compel children, through the juvenile justice system, to be law-abiding.

Sometimes the state may have to intervene in family affairs. When a child or parent is chemically dependent, the state may intervene in the areas of commitment for treatment, education, parental liability, and child abuse and neglect. We will discuss these issues in greater detail in other chapters. The state or federal government cannot, however, infringe on the rights of parents or children without "due process of law." This means all laws must be reasonable and related to a legitimate government purpose. Before a person is deprived of property, liberty, or other rights, that person is entitled to procedural fairness including the right to a fair hearing and counsel.[4]

Child Welfare

In addition to state welfare programs, the federal government provides a number of programs for needy families with children.[5] An example is Aid to Families with Dependent Children (AFDC), which is administered jointly by the federal and state governments. This program provides regular cash payments to needy parents or relatives who care for children in order to provide basic necessities. Application for AFDC is made at the local office of a state's welfare agency. People receiving AFDC are required to work or receive employment training, except those unable to do so, such as people who are alone and must care for minor children, or who are too ill or old to work.

Someone on AFDC, or any other federal welfare or disability program, is qualified to receive Medicaid, which is a joint federal/state program providing medical care financing. Medicaid should not be confused with Medicare, which is a program of hospitalization and medical benefits for persons who are over age 65 and on Social Security. People who receive Medicaid or Medicare may be able to use them to obtain chemical dependency treatment for themselves and/or their children.[6]

Juvenile Justice

Chemically dependent children who break the law have greater rights to treatment than do adults who commit crimes.[7] Children who break the law are brought before a juvenile court. Although the juvenile court works differently from an adult court, children are still afforded due process rights, as are adults.[8] Juvenile courts are empowered to hear cases involving *delinquency* and *status* offenses.[9] Delinquency occurs when a child commits an offense that would be a crime for an adult. A status offense is noncriminal behavior such as truancy, running away, or refusing to obey parental authority. Status offenders are deemed to be "in need of supervision." In delinquency cases, the court hears the matter in a regular court hearing and makes a formal resolution of the case. In status offenses, the court is less strict and will try to resolve matters informally. Status offenses account for at least one-third of the cases that come before the court.[10] In all states, the use of drugs by a minor is a matter of delinquency. In the case of alcohol use, it may only be a status offense or considered a minor delinquency charge. In both situations, rehabilitation is the primary aim of the juvenile court.

In the case of motor vehicle offenses, in most states juveniles will go to an adult court for trial and sentencing. They will receive the same sentences as adults would.

Drinking Age Laws

No area of juvenile justice has attracted more attention than drinking age laws.[11] The federal government is encouraging all the states to adopt 21 as the legal age to purchase alcoholic beverages, thereby having a national uniform drinking age.[12] The age of 21 has been a symbol of adulthood since medieval times, when at that age men were thought strong enough to wear heavy armor.[13] In modern times, we have given many rights of adulthood at age eighteen or lower ages. However, raising the drinking age to 21 has saved young lives by preventing alcohol-related motor vehicle accidents. The drinking age in your state is significant because it not only classifies underage drinkers as delinquents or status offenders, but it also classifies adults as criminals or liable for negligence if they serve or sell alcohol to minors.

Family Courts

In addition to the juvenile court system, some states have family courts, with broad powers to intervene when a family crisis exists, as in the case of an alcoholic parent or when a drug-abusing child is a constant runaway (see Chapter 5 on Treatment). A good way to find out how courts work in your state is to contact your local prosecutor's office, child welfare agency, or state alcohol and other drug agency. They can tell you what can be done to help chemically dependent children who break the law.

Chapter 3
ENDNOTES

1. *American Jurisprudence,* 2nd, ed., (Rochester, NY: The Lawyers' Cooperative Publishing Co., San Francisco, CA: Bancroft Whitney Co., 1971) 59, sec. 9-10; also Inge N. Dobelis, ed., *Reader's Digest Family Legal Guide* (Pleasantville, NY, 1981) p. 703.
2. *American Jurisprudence,* 59, sec. 9.
3. Tom Christoffel, *Health and the Law, A Handbook for Health Professionals* (New York: The Free Press, 1982) pp. 406-7.
4. Steven H. Gifis, *Law Dictionary* (Woodbury, NY: Barrons Educational Series, Inc., 1975) pp. 65-66.
5. *Reader's Digest Family Legal Guide,* pp. 1036-38.
6. For information on this program contact the Office of Research and Demonstrations, Health Care Financing Administration, Oak Meadows Bldg., 6340 Security Boulevard, Baltimore, Maryland 21207, and see Titles XVIII and XIX of the Social Security Act.
7. Alan A. Stone, M.D., *Mental Health and Law: A System in Transition, Crime and Delinquency Issues: A Monograph Series* (Rockville, MD: National Institute of Mental Health, Center for Studies of Crime and Delinquency, 1975-6) pp. 145-9.

8. *In re* Gault, 387 U.S. 1 (1967) Kent v. United States, 383 U.S. 541 (1966); *In re* Winship, 397 U.S. 358 (1970).
9. *Reader's Digest Family Legal Guide,* p. 603; see N.Y. 29A, Judiciary-Family Court sec. 712, and CAL Welfare and Institutions sec. 1-3999 (sec. 601) as examples.
10. *Reader's Digest Family Legal Guide,* p. 564.
11. Howard T. Blane and Morris E. Chafetz, *Youth, Alcohol and Social Policy* (New York: Plenum Press, 1979) pp. 240-3.
12. *Presidential Commission on Drunk Driving* (Washington, D.C.) (1983) U.S. Government Printing Office 1983-427-056- 814/233, p. 10; and *The U.S. Journal of Drug and Alcohol Dependence,* (Miami, FL, August, 1984), vol. 8, No. 8, p. 1.
13. *Reader's Digest Family Legal Guide,* p. 561.

IV
SCHOOLS

Alcohol and other drug abuse in schools endangers students, disrupts the educational process, and raises many questions regarding liability for teachers, school officials, and parents.[1] School officials and teachers feel particularly vulnerable when confronted with school drug abuse problems because they can get caught in a number of conflicts. For example, they may want to help and protect students who have problems, yet under certain circumstances they must report drug use by students to the principal or other authorities. If such reporting is required, students may not develop a sense of trust when talking to teachers or school counselors. What happens if a student overdoses on drugs while at school? Can the school take the student to emergency treatment, or do they have to get parental consent first? Suppose a school counselor tells a student that the student has an alcohol problem. Can the counselor be sued for libel or slander? The answers to these questions will be discussed throughout this book. This chapter will lay the foundation to answer these questions by giving you a good idea of the rights and responsibilities of schools, students, and parents.

This chapter discusses laws and issues relevant to elementary and high schools, both public and private. Since most college students are considered adults, except for the purchase of alcohol, most of the laws covered in this chapter will not apply to colleges.

Rights and Responsibilities of Schools

The basic unit of the public school system is the school district, which is created by an act of the state legislature. The school district is a geographic area and is governed by a school board usually composed of elected or appointed community members. The school board largely controls school policy; however, federal and state governments have a profound impact on local schools because they give money for local education and therefore claim a right to regulate certain aspects of school function.

Public schools have many legal powers. For example, attendance by students is mandatory, and truancy is an offense for a child and his or her parents. Schools also have the power to maintain discipline to ensure students' safety and to fulfill their educational goals.

In order to maintain discipline, schools can do a variety of things; the most common is a suspension from school. In private schools, students can be dismissed from school, which causes a forfeit of the money the parents paid for tuition.

Schools can also use corporal punishment, the striking or spanking of a child, to maintain discipline. While still in use in some private schools it is generally considered too harsh for public schools, although many states still authorize its use by public schools. The courts do not consider it cruel and unusual punishment as long as the child is not injured and the amount of force used is reasonable.[2]

Schools can set specific rules regarding student drug abuse.[3] State legislatures or municipal governments also pass laws regarding this issue, and very often these laws require teachers and other school officials to report cases of student drug abuse to the proper authorities. The laws that require reporting may relieve the teacher or school officials from any civil liability for doing so.[4]

Schools have rights, under certain circumstances, to search students or student lockers, especially if it is necessary to maintain school discipline or if there is reason to believe a student possesses drugs or a weapon.[5]

Civil Rights

School officials must protect a student's civil rights to equality in education and avoid discrimination based on race, color, religion, national origin, and sex. School officials, however, are entitled to a "good faith" immunity from liability under the Federal Civil Rights Act if they damage a student's civil rights by mistake or accident.[6]

Crimes

School officials may have a duty to report crimes under state or federal law. Check your state law. Under federal law, if you have knowledge of the actual commission of a federal felony, failure to report it can result in a fine or imprisonment.[7]

Lawsuits against Schools

The most common cause of major lawsuits against schools involve physical injuries to students which occur in school. Schools may be liable for such injuries or other torts, but not to the same degree as other entities. Years ago, schools were immune to such suits under the general theory of governmental immunity. This has been modified. Today, suits against schools are possible under special limits. For example, in many states, school boards must be notified of the intent to sue within 60-90 days after the injury. This differs from the one or two year time limit to start a lawsuit normally allowed by a state. This 60-90 day rule works to the school's benefit by preventing many lawsuits because people lose the right to sue after the time limit.

In order to win a school lawsuit, the plaintiff must show the injury was caused by the intentional or careless conduct of a teacher or school official. The law does not require that students be constantly supervised, only that supervision and care is reasonable. If conditions are as safe as possible, even sports injuries may not make schools liable.[8] The law generally holds that a teacher is not an insurer of the health, welfare, and safety of his or her students,[9] but teachers and school officials do have the duty to use reasonable care in the protection of a child and to anticipate danger to the child. Anticipation of danger means they must provide protection when they know, or have a reason to know, the student needs it. They must prepare to give protection if the need arises and to be vigilant about ascertaining the need for protection.[10] Teachers and school officials should act when they become aware of the use of alcohol or other drugs by students in school. If action is not taken and the student is harmed or harms others, the school, teacher, or official may be liable. In these cases, the law will consider whether the school personnel reasonably should have been aware of the use of alcohol or other drugs, whether they acted reasonably in dealing with it upon becoming aware, and whether their conduct contributed or caused any of the damage to the student or others.[11]

In most situations, parents cannot waive the above duties on the part of school officials or teachers. For example, parents who sign waivers or releases regarding their child's participation in school activities may not lose their right to sue if an injury occurs.

School officials generally cannot get into trouble by counseling students with drug abuse problems. Since most counseling does not involve touching a student or medical treatment, the liability in such situations is very low. Liability can occur when a student is intoxicated in school, or is in other medical danger and the school officials do the wrong thing, *or nothing,* and an injury occurs. If the child's life is in danger, save the life with or without parental consent for treatment.

Most states have laws regarding emergency treatment of minors. For example, in California a school official can provide or obtain reasonable medical treatment for an ill or injured child during school hours if the parents cannot be reached to give consent.[12] Other states have similar laws and may even specifically govern drug abuse situations.[13] In these situations, you may be more liable if you do nothing than if you take constructive action.

Handicapped Students

In addition to liability for student injuries, schools are liable for protecting the educational rights of handicapped students. While some states have laws regarding handicapped students, the primary law involved is the Federal Rehabilitation Act of 1973.[14] This law protects handicapped people from discrimination. Alcoholics and other drug addicts are included under the definition of *handicapped*.[15] The law provides that recipients of federal funds, which includes virtually all schools, cannot exclude a qualified handicapped individual, solely by reason of his or her handicap, from participation in or receipt of benefits from any program or activity receiving such federal assistance. This means that alcoholics and other drug addicts cannot be excluded from school or school activities solely because they are addicts. This law protects such students from being denied a chance to recover while enrolled in school. For example, if a student wanted to go into residential or outpatient treatment during the school year, he or she could not be suspended, segregated, or punished for seeking treatment.[16] The exception to this law might be students who create discipline problems or are dangerous.[17] Disciplinary measures can be used even if the alcohol or other drug problems were a factor.

The basic questions for schools in helping a chemically dependent child, or in making educational decisions regarding the child are, Are we treating this student in the same way we treat other students who are ill? and Are we giving this student every chance to complete his or her education on time in the least restrictive environment appropriate to the situation?[18]

In addition to the Federal Rehabilitation Act, there are other federal laws that provide for the identification, assessment, placement, and due-process rights of handicapped children.[19] School officials, teachers, students, and parents should learn about them.

Rights and Responsibilities of Parents

Parents are responsible for providing an education for their children until they reach a certain age. This means parents must comply with mandatory school attendance laws.

Parents also have rights. For example, parents must give consent before a child is treated medically. However, this may not apply in alcohol or other drug emergencies in school. See Chapter 5 on Treatment.

Parents also have the right, under the Federal Family Educational Rights and Privacy Act of 1974, to inspect their children's school records and to be given a hearing to correct any inaccurate, misleading, or inappropriate information.[20] Parents must also give their consent before the child's records can be released to anyone. This will be discussed further in Chapter 6 on Confidentiality.

Rights of Students

In addition to the right to an education, a student has constitutional rights such as free expression, as long as the student does not disrupt school discipline or infringe on the rights of others. In addition, students have due process rights in regard to discipline. The U.S. Supreme Court has held that "students facing temporary suspension from a public school have property and liberty interests that qualify for protection under the Due Process Clause of the Fourteenth Amendment" to the U.S. Constitution.[21] This includes the right to be informed of the nature of the charge leading to suspension, the right to an explanation of the evidence, and a right to a hearing to present his or her version of what happened. This should take place before the suspension, unless circumstances require the student's immediate removal, in which case the hearing will take place as soon as possible.

Students may also have the right to obtain treatment for drug abuse problems without parental consent.[22] In such cases, the minor may have the right to confidentiality protection as if he or she were an adult.[23] There is more on this in chapter 5 on treatment and in chapter 6 on confidentiality.

Student Assistance Programs

When a student has an alcohol or other drug abuse problem, the best way to protect the schools and the student is to establish a Student Assistance Program (SAP).[24] SAPs work in various ways, but the general idea is to provide an identification, referral, and counseling program for drug abusing students.

The SAP concept is based on a successful industrial program called the Employee Assistance Program (EAP). These programs identify troubled employees by becoming aware of an employee's poor work performance. If an employee is not performing adequately, the employee's supervisor makes a referral to an EAP counselor for an assessment. If the counselor feels there is a problem, the employee is referred to a professional for diagnosis and treatment.

SAPs work in a similar way. Teachers and other school personnel are trained to recognize student performance and behavior problems which indicate that the student is abusing alcohol or other drugs, or is consistently troubled in other ways. These problems include a drop in grades or quality of school work, troubles with peers, hostility, withdrawal, changes in appearance, changes in school activities, tardiness, moodiness, conflict with teachers and, of course, intoxication in school.[25]

School personnel, after documenting these behaviors, will make a referral to a SAP counselor or other persons responsible for such problems. The appropriate person can then make a *preassessment* to determine if the student's problem can be addressed within the educational setting or should be referred to an outside resource for help.[26] The preassessment will include information from school personnel and teachers, an interview with the student, and a review of any specific disciplinary or other action taken and the student's response.[27]

If the SAP counselor makes a preassessment that a chemical dependency problem exists, a referral should result. A preassessment is not a diagnosis; it merely indicates a problem of some kind. A properly qualified individual would decide if a serious problem exists.[28]

Preassessment does not usurp the role of the teacher or administrator in dealing with student discipline. It provides a system for responding to situations which persist in spite of school disciplinary procedures and which school personnel feel uncomfortable in addressing within the school context.[29]

A SAP program trains school personnel to make an early identification of problems and to take actions objectively, based on observable behavior. This protects schools from liability because it avoids inappropriate steps or inaction which might result in legal liability.[30]

SAPs and Confidentiality

If a student voluntarily seeks help from the SAP or is referred, should the SAP protect the student's privacy even to the point of not informing the parents? Some authorities claim that by preserving confidentiality, we encourage students to accept or get help before serious problems arise. They question if students would ask for help if they knew their parents would be informed. They argue that, in most cases, the parents will find out anyway because the role of the SAP is to involve parents by encouraging the student to be open with his or her parents. Other authorities assert that parents should always be informed because they are responsible for the child and can be more effective than anyone else in getting help for their child. (See Chapter 6 on Confidentiality.) These issues should be worked out by consulting the applicable law, and by getting the school, SAP, and parents to develop policies together.

Community Involvement in SAPs

The SAP should develop policies and procedures in coordination with school officials, teachers, SAP personnel, the school board, and parents' groups.[31] The policies and procedures should be communicated to all of the above to avoid misunderstandings and lawsuits.

Chapter 4
ENDNOTES

1. Gail G. Milgram, Ed.D., and Robert J. Pandina, Ph.D., "Educational Implications of Adolescent Substance Use," *Journal of Alcohol and Drug Education,* 26, No. 3 (Spring 1981). Gail G. Milgram, Ed.D., "Alcoholism in the Family, Implications for the School," *Focus on Alcohol and Drug Issues* The U.S. Journal of Drug and Alcohol Dependence, Inc. (1981). James L. Malfetti, Ed.D., "Development of a Junior High School Module in Alcohol Education and Traffic Safety" (New York: Safety Research and Education Project, Teachers College, Columbia University, 1977).
2. Inge N. Dobelis, ed., *Reader's Digest Family Legal Guide,* (Pleasantville, NY, 1981) p. 857.
3. *Offenses and Dispositions,* Student Discipline Brochure; Dekalb County School System, 770 North Decatur Rd., Decatur, GA, 30032 (1982-3); also contact Families In Action, Suite 300, 3845 N. Druid Hills Rd., Decatur, GA 30033.

Kids, Drugs, and the Law

4. Florida Statues s. 232.277; Official Code of Georgia Annotated, 51-1-30.2; and see N.J.S.A. 18A:40-4.1,2; N.J.S.A. 2C:33-15,16.
5. People v. Jackson, 319 NY Supp. 2d 731; U.S. v. Rabinowitz, 339 U.S. 56 (1950); State v. McKinnon, 558 P. 2d 781 (1977); State v. Mora, 307 S 2d, 317 (1975); State in the Interest of T.L.O. 463 A 2d 934 (1983) and *In re* T.L.O. no. 83- 712, U.S. Supreme Ct. Jan. 15, 1985 (53 U.S.L.W. 4083, Jan. 15, 1985); Katz v. United States, 389 U.S. 347 (1967).
6. Thomas M. Griffin and Roger H. Svendsen, *The Role of the School in Responding to Chemical Health Issues and Problems* (Minnesota Department of Education, Division of Instruction, 1980), p. 10.
7. 18 U.S.C. sec. 4.
8. *Reader's Digest Family Legal Guide,* p. 856.
9. Grosso v. Wittemann, 62 N.W. 2d 386 (1954).
10. Grosso v. Wittemann above; and Restatement of the Law of Torts, Vol II sec. 320, p. 868; and Bogust v. Iverson, 102 N.W. 2d 228 (1960).
11. Griffin and Svendson, *The Role of the School in Responding to Chemical Health Issues and Problems,* pp. 10.
12. Cal. Educ. Code, sec. 49407, 76407 (West 1978).
13. N.J.S.A. 18A:40-4.1; Ariz. Rev. Stat. Ann. Section 44-133(1967); NC General Stat. Ann. Sections 90-21.1 to 90-21.4 (1975 Repl. Vol.); for a good general discussion on this topic see Arnold J. Rosoff, *Informed Consent, A Guide for Health Care Providers* (Rockville MD: Aspen Systems Corporation, 1981) p. 188.
14. Minnesota Statutes 120.17, and 120.03, Subd. 3., and Public Law 93-112, and Public Law 93-516; Title 29 U.S.C., Section 701 et seq.; see also Federal Register, May 4, 1977 Part IV and May 1, 1978, Part II.
15. Attorney General Opinion, Griffin Bell 1977; Appendix A following 45 CFR 84.61 at subpart A4, p. 290; also 41

CFR 60-741 (July 6, 1977); see also for a full discussion of the Rehabilitation Act of 1973, David G. Evans, *A Practitioner's Guide to Alcoholism and the Law* (Center City MN: Hazelden, 1983) pp. 57-65; and Gerald T. Hannah, Walter P. Christian, and Hewitt B. Clark, *Preservation of Client Rights* (New York: The Free Press 1981) pp. 61-5.

16. Hannah, Christian, and Clark, p. 64.
17. 29 USCA sec. 706 (7) (b).
18. Hannah, Christian, and Clark, p. 64.
19. Ibid., pp. 61-82; see also Public Law 93-380 an amendment to the Elementary and Secondary Education Act of 1965; and Education of All Handicapped Children Act, 20 U.S.C. sec. 1401, 1411. (see Federal Register August 23, 1977); see also *Summary of Federal Statutes and Regulations Concerning Children Requiring Special Education,* (Cambridge, MA: Center for Law and Education, Inc. 1980).
20. Sec. 438. Public Law 90-247, Title IV, as amended, 88 stat. 571-574 (20 U.S.C.: 1232 g); also 41 FR 24670, June 17, 1976; and Title 45 Public Welfare, Subtitle A, Department of Health and Human Services.
21. Robert E. Phay, *The Law of Procedure in Student Suspensions and Expulsion,* (Topeka, KS: National Organization of Legal Problems of Education, 1977); Goss v. Lopez, 419 U.S. 565 (1975); Morrisey v. Brewer, 408 U.S. 471 (1972); Dixon v. Alabama State Board of Ed., 294 F 2d 150 (5th Cir. 1961); *In re* Gault, 387 U.S. 1 (1967); Tinker v. Des Moines Ind. Comm. School Dist., 393 U.S. 503 (1969).
22. *Informed Consent,* pp. 187-231.
23. 42 CFR Part 2, Sec. 2.15.
24. Tom Griffin and Roger Svendsen, *The Student Assistance Program: How It Works* (Center City, MN: Hazelden, 1980).

25. Richard Neuner, *Preassessment Services Within The School: A Guide for Administrators, Teachers and Service Staff,* (Anoka, MN: Minnesota Institute, 1982), p. 7.
26. Ibid., p. 4.
27. Ibid., pp. 4, 7.
28. Ibid., p. 4.
29. Ibid., p. 6.
30. Ibid., p. 4.
31. *Prevention Plus: Involving Schools, Parents and the Community in Alcohol and Drug Education,* (Rockville, MD: U.S. Department of Health and Human Services, DHHS Publication No. (ADM) 83-1256, 1983); see also generally Griffin and Svendsen, *The Student Assistance Program.*

V
TREATMENT

Chemical dependency treatment for minors raises a number of legal issues. What about a minor's right to treatment, with or without parental consent? What rights do children and parents have to decide if treatment will be initiated and continued? Can parents force children to go to treatment? What legal pitfalls should treatment providers consider? What are the legal aspects of diagnosis? How should suicidal or dangerous patients be handled? This chapter will deal with these issues and explain the basic legal concepts so you can use or change your local laws.

Right to Consent to Treatment

What are the rights of parents or a child to consent to chemical dependency treatment for the child? This issue is important because many treatment providers and schools are afraid to provide treatment without parental consent. This fear is unwarranted because parental consent for chemical dependency treatment is often not required.

The law favors providing chemical dependency treatment for children. In fact, Washington D.C. and over 35 states specifically give juveniles the right to obtain alcohol or other drug treatment without requiring parental consent.[1] These laws vary widely as to who can provide treatment and types of permissible treatment, and some even exempt physicians from any civil or criminal liability for non-negligent treatment

37

of chemical dependency in minors.[2] These laws generally divide into three categories: those allowing children of any age to consent, those allowing minors of only certain ages to consent, and those leaving it to the discretion of treatment personnel to obtain parental consent.[3]

Many of the laws permit notification of the parents if notification would be helpful. However, in some states, if the treatment provider feels the child would not stay in treatment if the parents were notified, the provider can choose not to notify the parents. In most cases the parents can be informed, and treatment providers should work toward this.

Why does the law give minors the right to consent to treatment for chemical dependency? In the past, only parents were given the right to consent to medical treatment of their children.[4] This was based on the idea that children were the property of the parents, and therefore they could only be touched by medical personnel with parental consent. Current law still holds that subjecting a child to surgery without parental consent is a *battery* or an *assault,* i.e., an unlawful touching.[5] In addition, the law holds that children should be protected by parents because children lack experience or understanding.[6]

In recent years, these general rules have been modified. We now no longer see children as the property of parents. The law is now tending to see minors as persons and the law recognizes that children also have constitutional rights.[7] In addition, the law recognizes that certain medical problems of children must be dealt with separately, by giving children the right to consent to treatment so they will be encouraged to enter treatment. Such problems usually include venereal disease, chemical dependency, pregnancy, mental illness, and emergency treatment.[8] These problems are dealt with separately because young people who are living with their parents are often reluctant to face the breakdown of communication and the disruption that may occur if they tell their parents about such medical problems. These children may choose to go untreated, rather than have parents or school authorities find out. We need to encourage children to seek help in every possible way, and then work with them to get their families involved.

Mature Minor Rule

Even when there is no state right to treatment law for minors, it may still be proper to provide non-negligent medical treatment of a child over age fifteen who asks for and knowingly consents to treatment. In law, this is called the *mature minor rule* and has even applied in cases involving surgery.[9] In some states, a minor over fifteen with a chemical dependency problem who asks for treatment may be held to be legally competent to give treatment consent.[10] In such cases, a physician who refuses to provide treatment to a chemically dependent mature minor may be acting improperly.[11]

The mature minor rule applies when a minor is "sufficiently intelligent and mature to understand the nature and consequences of the medical treatment being sought."[12] The factors a court may use in deciding if a minor is mature are age, intelligence, training, experience, economic independence or lack thereof, general conduct as an adult, and freedom from the control of parents.[13]

Where chemical dependency treatment only involves outpatient counseling, it is easy to see how children fifteen or older would be considered mature minors for this type of treatment. However, inpatient treatment, surgery, the prescription of drugs, or risky or intrusive treatments are other issues.

Valid Consent

If a state uses a mature minor rule or has a minor's right to treatment law, what factors might the law consider in deciding whether the child's consent is valid and the treatment program acted properly? The first factor is the age of the child. If the child is at least fifteen years old, the law may hold that he or she is old enough to understand treatment procedures and to appreciate their risks. If the minor is nearer to the age of majority, his or her consent is given even more weight.[14] The law may also consider whether the child actually consented or gave implied consent, whether the treatment was necessary and for the child's benefit only, and the degree of risk involved in the treatment.[15] In addition, the law may consider whether there was a good reason, including a minor's refusal to contact parents, why parental consent was not or could not be obtained.[16] The law may also consider whether the child is emancipated and/or married or in the military service.[17]

The law may look to see whether the child was under any influence to consent and whether the consent was *informed.* Informed consent, depending on state law, generally means the patient has an "informed exercise of choice," which "entails an opportunity to evaluate knowledgeably the options available and the risks attendant upon each."[18] This means the treatment provider may have to disclose to the patient the diagnosis of the patient's problem, the nature and purpose of the treatment proposed, the risks and consequences of treatment, the probability of the treatment's success, feasible treatment alternatives, and prognosis if the treatment is not given.[19]

Qualified Treatment

If a state uses a mature minor rule or gives a minor the right to consent, does it apply to all types of chemical dependency treatment and all types of chemical dependency professionals? In most cases, these laws apply only to medical treatment and/or treatment supervised by a physician, or other licensed professional or state agencies. They may not apply to unlicensed paraprofessionals, or untrained volunteer-staffed programs.[20] Check your state law on this issue. It is probably safe to say that an unlicensed program, staffed by unqualified persons, cannot be as well-protected as professionally staffed and licensed programs. This would be especially true if the unlicensed or unqualified programs used a type of therapy outside the normal range of treatment.

Parental Consent Issues for Treatment Providers

In deciding when to get parental consent, first check your
state law regarding children's treatment rights. Generally, all
laws involving children should be interpreted as benefitting
the child. The Supreme Court has often held that a child may
only be dealt with differently from an adult by a governmental
entity if the result is of benefit to the child.[21]

Your state may not apply a minor's right to treatment law
or the mature minor rule for children under fifteen. In such
cases, it is wise to obtain parental consent for all treatment.
Consult your attorney about this.

If your state clearly requires parental consent, a treatment
provider should not administer treatment without it. The only
exceptions would be emergency situations or as otherwise
allowed by your state law. Check this with your attorney.
Most states have laws permitting emergency medical treatment
of children when parental consent cannot be obtained.[22] The
treating physician will not be liable if the treatment was
proper. In addition, every state has a "Good Samaritan" law
to protect people who render aid in emergency situations.

If parents are divorced or separated, and parental consent is
needed for nonemergency treatment, go to the parent who has
custody of the child. If the custodial parent is not available,
consent may be obtained from the other parent. If the parents
are not available, a treatment provider can seek consent from
someone who stands *in loco parentis* or otherwise has the
power to give consent. A temporary custodian, such as an
older sister, may not have this power.[23] In a nonemergency
setting, it is best to wait to get parental or *in loco parentis*
consent prior to treatment.

What if a parent refuses to consent to needed treatment?
Can treatment providers seek legal authorization for treatment? If treatment is needed, all states have legal procedures
to authorize medical care in appropriate cases, even over the
objection of parents.[24] These laws allow providers to seek

court orders to render treatment. It also may be possible to render emergency treatment against parents' wishes without a court order. However, such actions place providers at risk if they cannot later justify the action. The best way to protect yourself is to develop procedures and criteria for such treatment before an emergency. Your attorney can help you develop these guidelines.

The Issue of Children's Right to Treatment

Some people argue that children should have no right to consent to treatment. They feel parents should always control the situation, including refusing treatment for a child who wants it. They believe parents are responsible for their children and this responsibility should not be taken away from them. They assert that in most cases the child does not want treatment and parents are the ones who initiate the treatment contact.

Others argue that children should have rights to enter treatment because a decision to enter treatment is a good one, and we should encourage children to make such decisions. They feel some children would otherwise never get a chance to enter treatment because they are unable to get help from their parents, or because parents will deny the child's problem and refuse to let the child enter a program. There is also the situation where parents may be alcohol or other drug abusers themselves and will not support the child's desire to get help.

Both sides in this discussion have valid points of view. These issues are important and should be resolved by a balanced solution. For example, in those states where children do not have the right to enter treatment, parents should have the right to commit or otherwise help a child into treatment. In those states where parents have all rights, some procedure should be available to help children when their parents do not want it for them.

When the Child Needs Help but Refuses It

If a child needs help but refuses it, the child should be forced into it, as any proper treatment is better than no treatment. If the treatment program staff is competent, they will know how to help the child get well.

The first issue for parents is to decide if the child really needs treatment. The best way to know is to seek the opinion of a qualified chemical dependency professional. Not all physicians, psychiatrists, psychologists, or counselors are properly trained in chemical dependency. Parents should locate one who is knowledgeable. Some of these professionals will be certified alcoholism or other drug abuse counselors. You can locate these experts in your state by consulting your state alcohol and other drug agency or by contacting the National Association of Alcoholism and Drug Abuse Counselors.[25] In addition, your state agency will help locate parents' groups and other self-help groups that can give you information and support.

Once you have decided your child needs help, there are many ways to persuade your child to accept it. Chemical dependency professionals and programs that treat children are often very skilled at this and can counsel you and your child. Sometimes a process called *intervention* is necessary where the family and trained counselors confront the child together in a loving, but firm way.

If your state gives minors the right to consent to alcohol or other drug treatment without parental consent, does this mean minors have the right to refuse treatment? This is an issue to be decided by your state law. Laws of this type should be interpreted to benefit the child. If the child needs help and the parents want help for the child, these laws should not be a barrier to treatment.[26]

With all of this in mind, if you have no choice, use legal force. Your child's life may depend on it.

Legal Force

If all your efforts at counseling and persuasion do not work and you believe your child's life is in danger, you may choose to use the law to get your child into treatment. The three major tools are the juvenile court, the family court, and your state's commitment laws. This should be a last resort, because the attorneys or judges who handle the case may not be knowledgeable in chemical dependency problems. A court could force your child into inappropriate treatment or enable the child to stay sick by not properly confronting the child.

Juvenile Court

Parents can use the juvenile court by filing a complaint against a child for a crime, for *incorrigibility,* or some similar offense where a child does not respond to lawful parental authority. When filing such complaints, it is crucial that parents ensure the child is evaluated for alcohol or other drug problems and the court orders treatment if needed. If the child refuses treatment or continues to misbehave, the next logical step is for the court to order the child incarcerated or punished in some other way. For many parents, the use of the juvenile court would be a last step because of the potential seriousness of the above consequences and because it results in a criminal record for the child.

Family Court

Another approach parents can use is the family court. Not all states have such a court, but if your state does, you can petition the court to resolve a family crisis. If the court hears the petition, the court can order family members into treatment. This is a civil procedure and does not give anyone a criminal record.

For example, one state allows its family court to hear cases where "a member of a family alleges that some other member

of the family is by his conduct imperiling any family relationship and petitions the Court for appropriate relief."[27] Another
state allows its family court to get involved in a *Juvenile-
Family Crisis* which is in part defined as "a serious conflict
between a parent or guardian and a juvenile regarding rules
of conduct which has been manifested by a repeated disregard
for lawful parental authority by a juvenile," which includes
running away and truancy.[28]

Commitment

Another legal technique is to commit your child under your
state's commitment law. Most states will allow a commitment
specifically for alcohol or other drug abuse.[29] Please note that
due process requires the child be given a hearing on the need
for commitment. On this issue the courts have held that
parents cannot decide on their own that a child should be
committed and "that the risk of error inherent in the parental
decision to have a child institutionalized for mental health
care is sufficiently great that some kind of inquiry should be
made by a *neutral fact finder* to determine whether the
statutory requirements for admission are satisfied."[30] It is not
required that this fact finder be a judge, however he or she
must have the power to refuse to admit the child if the medical
standards for admission are not met. If the child is admitted,
the need for continuing commitment must be reviewed periodi-
cally.[31]

All the above procedures require due process.[32] Parents
attempting to use them should be prepared to present evidence
of their child's problems. Such evidence can include a physician's or therapist's evaluation, school reports, and testimony
of family and friends.

Financial Liability of Parents and Children

In most instances, including emergencies, parents are liable
for their children's medical expenses. However, this may not

be true if a minor has the right to be treated as an adult, and/or the parents did not authorize treatment. Depending on state law, the minor may be liable for the expense, or the program or government may have to absorb the cost.[33] If a treatment program is publicly supported and offers free services, then a minor who has a right to treatment may not have to pay.[34]

Diagnosis

Who is legally qualified to diagnose chemical dependency in a child? How should a diagnosis be performed? These questions may arise when a parent, child, attorney, or judge disagrees with the evaluation of a school counselor or treatment professional and challenges the professional's evaluation or diagnosis. For example, a parent might say about the child, "He's not a drug addict! He's just having a good time," or, "He's just experimenting."

In looking at this issue, let us first consider the word *diagnosis*. According to *Webster's Dictionary*, it is "the art or process of deciding the nature of a diseased condition by examination of the symptoms."[35] This definition does not indicate a diagnosis has to be done by a professional. Anyone can make a diagnosis. But how well will the diagnosis stand up if it is challenged? For example, a diagnosis by a psychiatrist who uses the standardized diagnostic techniques recognized by the medical profession will have greater authority in a court than the diagnosis of an untrained paraprofessional. On the other hand, the psychiatrist may know nothing about chemical dependency and may diagnose the child as *neurotic,* as having *adolescent adjustment reaction,* or another behavioral disorder. The paraprofessional may have years of experience and spot the problem right off. Testimony from paraprofessional counselors with years of experience often stands up better in court than that of some professionals. The knowledge they displayed made them credible experts. However, if a treatment program or school is concerned about challenges to its diagnosis of children, the ideal situation would be to have it done by a licensed professional who is thoroughly trained in chemical dependency.

If you are not such a professional or don't have access to one, and yet you are in a position where you must make a diagnosis, perhaps it would be better to call the diagnosis an *evaluation.* Somehow the term *evaluation* is less loaded and is easier for people to accept. We will use *diagnosis* because it is more frequently used in law.

Guidelines for Diagnosis

If you are a professional or paraprofessional, you should use the following guidelines in performing a diagnosis:

(1) *Make a careful examination of the patient.*[36] Do the evaluation personally, and make sure that you do not make "snap" judgments. Do not rely on the word of others, and make sure the patient gives you complete information.[37]

(2) *Utilize standardized diagnostic tests.*[38] If you use such tests and you are trained in their use, your diagnosis will be easier to defend. If you use reasonable care in arriving at a diagnosis and make a reasonable judgment call, even if it is in error, you may not be liable.

To diagnose chemical dependency in a young person, the most recognized devices are

a. *The Diagnostic and Statistical Manual of Mental Disorders (DSM III),* published by the American Psychiatric Association.[39] The DSM III has a section on alcohol and other drug abuse disorders.

b. The Adolescent Alcohol Involvement Scale.[40]

c. The Michigan Alcoholism Screening Test (MAST) and the Mortimer-Filkens test, which were developed for adults.[41]

d. The McAndrews Scale on the Minnesota Multiphasic

Personality Inventory.[42] The MMPI can give you an overall personality picture, as well as information on tendencies towards addiction.

These and various other devices and criteria for diagnosis can be obtained from your state alcohol and other drug agency or from the sources listed in the endnotes to this chapter.[43]

In addition to the above, *every* state has a statutory definition of alcoholism and/or other drug abuse which can be used as part of a diagnosis.[44] Check your local law library.

Whether a minor can consent to a diagnostic test is an issue that often arises. Diagnosis for chemical dependency rarely involves any procedure that involves physical risk or discomfort. Therefore, the possibility of damage to the child is practically nonexistent, and the liability of treatment providers is very low.[45] What happens if the diagnostic test result is incorrect, and upon being told the diagnosis the patient develops emotional problems as a result? This is called an *iatrogenic disorder* and could make the provider liable, but only if the diagnosis was negligently determined.[46] Such cases usually involve incorrect diagnoses of diseases such as cancer, and the person suffers a breakdown as a result. If the provider performed a correct diagnostic procedure and made a mistake in judgment, there may be no liability. Of course, if the diagnosis was correct, there would be no liability. In any case, unless there was severe injury to the patient, it is unlikely the provider would be made to pay damages.

(3) The final guideline is that *you should keep the diagnosis confidential* and only release it in accordance with state and federal laws, rules, and regulations that govern your situation. (See Chapter 6 on Confidentiality.)

Defamation and Treatment

If you follow proper confidentiality procedures, you will save yourself a lot of trouble, including a possible suit for defamation. Defamation occurs when you speak, publish, write, or otherwise communicate anything untrue that injures a person's personal reputation or business reputation.[47] The two forms of defamation are *libel* and *slander.*

Libel occurs when you write or print a false and malicious statement about a person that exposes that person to public ridicule or scorn.[48] You do not have to prove that the person was damaged by it; the publication of the statement is considered damage enough. The libel laws also apply to the press, although their liability is somewhat limited.[49]

Slander occurs when you make an untrue oral remark about a person that damages his or her reputation.[50] In slander cases, though, it must be proved the person was actually financially or otherwise damaged by the statement, or that the slander affected the person's business.[51] Please note: in order to constitute a libel or slander case, the statement must be untrue.

Privilege as a Defense to Defamation

In some circumstances, even if you say or write an untrue statement about a person, you may have protection from suit. This is called a *privilege.* There are two general types of privilege — *absolute* and *qualified.*[52] An absolute privilege is usually extended to persons acting in a governmental function, such as a witness or attorney in court, or a legislator. The public interest lies in having complete freedom of speech in this context. Qualified privilege is when the public interest protects people who make communications in good faith, without malice, and when they have a proper purpose or legitimate social duty for releasing the information. In addition, the disclosure must be limited in scope to what is necessary to perform the legitimate purpose or social duty, and the disclosure must be made only to the appropriate parties with a right to know.[53] Qualified privilege may be lost if a person does not act reasonably, performs in a reckless or wanton way, and causes injury.[54] The qualified privilege may apply even when an untrue statement is made by mistake or caused by inexperience.[55]

It appears that treatment providers, school counselors, and other professionals would come under this qualified privilege if they acted in a reasonable manner to help a child or to further some similar social duty. For example, it may apply when a teacher reports to a principal that a student is intoxicated in school, or when a counselor reports a dangerous patient to the police. Even if the information were untrue, the qualified privilege may apply if the above criteria are met.

Consent as a Defense to Defamation

Another protection from liability for libel and slander is *consent*.[56] Consent occurs when the person agrees that the statements about him or her can be communicated. If a treatment provider obtains written consent from a patient before releasing information on the patient, the provider would have a very strong defense if the patient later sued, claiming an improper release of information.[57]

It is plain that following proper confidentiality procedures not only protects the patient, it protects the treatment provider and school counselor from getting sued for libel or slander. If they follow proper confidentiality procedures, they may fall under the qualified privilege rule. Check your state law.

The Dangerous Patient

If you are a school counselor or treatment professional and you have a chemically dependent child patient who is dangerous, and who you believe will harm another, you should take whatever steps are necessary to warn any potential victims, unless there is a law that specifically says you cannot.

A treatment provider might ask four questions about this general rule: (1) How do I know a person is dangerous? (2) Why do I have a duty to warn? (3) What are the necessary steps I must take to warn? and (4) What laws govern these situations?

Situations where you will have to warn a victim are very rare. However, this issue has received a lot of publicity and it should be addressed.

Let us first look at how a provider should know whether a patient is dangerous. If you are a psychiatrist, psychologist, or other counseling professional, most likely the law will presume you have this knowledge. If you do not have it, and you deal with potentially dangerous patients, you had best receive additional training. If you are a volunteer counselor, with no professional training, you may not be presumed to have this special knowledge. In any case, common sense should rule. If a patient tells you he or she is going to hurt somebody, you do not need to be a trained professional to assume a potential danger exists. Beyond obvious threats, there are other signs of danger such as statements of violent intentions, a history of violent behavior, an inability to feel and express concern for others, impulsiveness and poor capacity for self-control, and any physical or neurological dysfunction.[58]

Again, use common sense. If a patient makes a statement such as, "Sometimes I get so mad at my teacher I could just kill him," that alone may not be enough to warn of danger. We all get hostile feelings from time to time, and therapy is a place to work them out. If you have a situation you are unsure of, ask for help, and discuss your concern with competent professionals.

If you believe your patient is dangerous, what should you do? First, why do you have a duty to do anything at all? Why should you try to control the patient's behavior? People usually have no duty to warn victims or control the behavior of others. As a therapist or counselor, however, you may have a legally recognized *special relationship* with the patient that gives you a duty to control or take actions regarding that person.[59] This duty is based on your special knowledge of

51

human behavior, which gives you the ability to be aware of danger and to foresee risk. Since you are aware when others are not, you have a duty to warn. This special knowledge may give you the power to take actions to have the person detained by the police and other authorities and be committed for observation and treatment. Again, it depends on your professional status; a physician has the power to commit, a volunteer counselor may not. If a physician knows of a person's dangerousness and does not take action to warn and/or commit, the physician may be liable. A volunteer counselor may be liable to a lesser extent, if at all.

Once you decide you have a dangerous patient and you must warn possible victims, make sure you go all the way. Half measures will avail you nothing. In the leading case in this area, a therapist who had a dangerous patient and who knew the identity of the victim, tried to prevent the victim's death by having the patient detained by the police for a commitment proceeding. The patient talked the police out of it and never went back to the therapist. Two months later, the patient killed the victim.

What should the therapist have done? The court held that the victim or her parents should have been directly warned. This could have been done by the therapist, or the therapist could have ensured the police or other authorities did it. In this case, the court held there was a duty to warn because the therapist was a professional, the patient was clearly dangerous, and the victim was known.[60]

What laws govern confidentiality in these situations? (See Chapter 6 on Confidentiality.) The Federal Alcohol and Drug Confidentiality Regulations do not speak directly to this point, however, under these regulations you could provide an anonymous warning, or seek a court order, or declare it a bona fide medical emergency and release the information. There may also be state laws that apply. Your state will have various statutory laws, regulations, or court rules governing the confidentiality of the patient-physician relationship and/

or the patient relationship with other therapists or counselors. These confidentiality requirements may mention what to do about dangerous patients, or they may forbid you to reveal information, even in dangerous situations. It is possible your state has a law saying your duty to preserve confidentiality is more important than your duty to warn.[61] Consult your attorney for a legal opinion.

What do you do if the law in your state is not clear? If there are no clear guidelines and you have to make a choice, choose on the side of giving a warning if this action is necessary to prevent a death or injury. The warning should be done in a professional, organized way. If time permits, consult with a mental health professional and an attorney. You must warn only those persons necessary to protect any potential victim. If a therapist acts in good faith and the warning is based on real facts of the patient's dangerousness, if the victim is known, and if the release of information was limited to a need to know, it is hard to see how the law would hold a therapist liable, even if a mistake was made.

Suicidal Children

Treatment providers may be liable if they do not take steps to protect suicidal children. This can occur if the provider should have known that the person was suicidal and failed to diagnose, made a negligent diagnosis, or if the provider became aware but did not respond adequately.[62] In some rare cases, it is possible the acts of the provider could have contributed to a suicide by breaching a confidence, improper prescription of drugs, termination of treatment prematurely, or by giving advice that precipitates a suicide.[63]

The first issue to consider is whether the provider knew, or should have known, of the potential suicide. Was the risk foreseeable? Liability will depend on how obvious the evidence of suicide was and on how professionally qualified the provider was. An untrained volunteer would not be expected to detect the subtle signs of suicide, as would a psychiatrist. However, even a program using an untrained volunteer would be responsible if the signs of suicide were obvious and the program took no steps. Obvious signs of potential suicide are suicide threats or expressions from the patient that suicide is being considered. All chemical dependency programs should be aware of how to detect and take action regarding suicides, since it is foreseeable that addicted persons will become depressed. *You will be more liable for failure to act, than to act. So act!*

There are many ways of detecting and diagnosing suicidal persons.[64] If you obtain this information and follow the diagnostic guidelines discussed earlier, you will protect yourself. One good way of obtaining information is to seek training from your local mental health agency. *All* chemical dependency treatment personnel should receive this basic training, and all professionals should be trained to handle this problem in accordance with the standards of their profession.

Once you have detected a potentially suicidal patient, and if you are qualified to provide treatment, do so. If you are not, seek qualified assistance. When in doubt, ask for help. Unless you are trained and qualified to handle all suicidal situations, do not decide on your own that the patient is bluffing or manipulating. Get help, and make sure you do not abandon the patient. It is your responsibility to follow through with the patient until he or she receives proper care.[65] Just referring someone to a qualified professional may not be enough. You should see to it that the professional is properly informed of the situation.[66]

What about confidentiality? As with dangerous patients, you have to check your state and federal confidentiality laws; however, chances are that you can breach confidentiality if the danger is imminent and if the communication is done in a proper way, based on a need to know. When in doubt, take action to save the life. If you do it properly, as we discussed

in the dangerous patient section — even if you make a diagnostic mistake — you may be safe from liability.

This chapter has covered some treatment liability issues
specific to young people. There are other liability issues that
apply in all treatment situations for adults and young people.
These issues have been discussed in my book *A Practitioner's
Guide to Alcoholism and the Law,* published by Hazelden.
The book has chapters on malpractice, confidentiality, criminal law, family law, discrimination, employment law, and
testifying in court as well as a chapter for attorneys.[67]

Chapter 5
ENDNOTES

1. Arnold J. Rosoff, *Informed Consent, A Guide for
   Health Care Providers,* (Rockville, MD: Aspen Systems
   Corporation, 1981) pp. 211-31.
2. See Kentucky R.S. Diseases sec. 214. 185 (1) p. 89;
   Kansas S.A. Public Health sec. 65-2892 (g). p. 238; and
   Ann. Code of Maryland, Act. 43 sec. 135 enacted 1967
   amended 1977; and Robert A. Rombro, J.D., LL.M.,
   Minor's Capacity to Consent to Medical Treatment (MD
   Stat. Med. J. February 1978).
3. Eugene I. Pavalon, *Human Rights and Health Care Law*
   (New York: American Journal of Nursing Co. Education
   Services Division, 1980) p. 124.
4. Arnold O. Ginnow and George Gordon, eds., *Corpus
   Juris Secundum* (St. Paul, MN: West Publishing Co.) 67
   A, Parent and Child, sec. 10 and 11; and see generally,
   John M. McCabe, Esq., *Child's Consent to Treatment,*
   Report prepared for the National Institute on Alcohol
   Abuse and Alcoholism, (Rockville, MD: NIAAA, 1977).
5. Bonner v. Moran, 126 F. 2d 121; and Lacy v. Laird, 139
   N.E. 2d 25.
6. Pavalon, *Human Rights and Health Care Law,* pp. 117-
   19.

Kids, Drugs, and the Law

7. Ibid., p. 118; see also Jenkins, "Rights of Children," *Fordham Law Review* 46:669, 671, 1978.
8. Pavalon, *Human Rights and Health Care Law,* p. 118; and Rosoff, *Informed Consent, A Guide for Health Care Providers* pp. 192-4.
9. Angela Roddey Holder, LL.M., *Legal Issues in Pediatrics and Adolescent Medicine* (New York: John Wiley and Sons, 1977) p. 145; see also Harriet S. Pilpel, *Minor's Rights to Medical Care,* 36 Albany Law Rev., pp. 472-87, 466; and Pavalon, *Human Rights and Health Care Law,* pp. 123- 126
10. Holder, *Legal Issues in Pediatrics and Adolescent Medicine,* p. 143.
11. Ibid.
12. Pavalon, *Human Rights and Health Care Law,* p. 123; see also Paul, "Legal Rights of Minors to Sex Related Medical Care," *Colorado Human Rights Law Review,* 6:357 (1974- 5).
13. Pavalon, *Human Rights and Health Care Law,* p. 123; see also Smith v. Seibly, 72 Wash. 2d 16, 431 P 2d 719 at 723 (1967).
14. Holder, *Legal Issues in Pediatrics and Adolescent Medicine,* p. 146.
15. Ibid., p. 146; see also Bonner v. Moran, 126 F 2d 123 (D.C. Cir. 1941).
16. Holder, *Legal Issues in Pediatrics and Adolescent Medicine,* p. 146.
17. Pavalon, *Human Rights and Health Care Law,* pp. 117-19, 121-33.
18. Schloendorff v. Society of New York Hospital, 464 F 2d 772, 780 (D.C. Cir. 1972).
19. Rosoff, *Informed Consent, A Guide for Health Care Providers,* p. 41; and David G. Evans, *A Practitioner's Guide to Alcoholism and the Law,* (Center City, MN: Hazelden, 1983) p. 15.

20. Holder, *Legal Issues in Pediatrics and Adolescent Medicine,* p. 241.
21. Ibid., p. 136; see also *In re* Gault 387 U.S. 1 (1967).
22. Holder, *Legal Issues in Pediatrics and Adolescent Medicine,* p. 138; and Rosoff, *Informed Consent, A Guide for Health Care Providers,* p. 188; Marguerite R. Mancini and Alice T. Gale, *Emergency Care and The Law* (Rockville, MD: Aspen Systems (Orp. 1981), pp. 55-6.
23. Rosoff, *Informed Consent, A Guide for Health Care Providers,* p. 194.
24. Ibid., p. 194.
25. NAADAC's address is 951 South George Mason Dr., Arlington, VA, 22204, Phone (703) 920-4644.
26. Holder, *Legal Issues in Pediatrics and Adolescent Medicine,* p. 246; see also *In re* Smith 295 A 2nd 238, MD, 1972.
27. Delaware Code, Title 10, Chapter 9 sec. 921.
28. N.J.S. 2 A: 4 A 22 (g).
29. Most states have a separate commitment law for alcoholism or other drug addiction. The states with no separate commitment law for alcoholism are AL, AR, AK, ID, KY, MI, MO, NE, NV, NH, NY, OH, OR, PA, SD, VT, WA, WV, and WY. Those with no separate commitment law for other drugs are AR, CO, DE, ID, IL, KS, MA, MI, MO, MT, NV, NJ, NM, NY, OH, OR, PA, RI, SD, WA, WV, and WY. In all the above states you may be able to commit under the state mental health law for alcohol or other drugs if the mental health requirements are met.
30. Parham v. J.R., 442 U.S. 584-5, 1979; and McCabe, *Child's Consent to Treatment,* p. 17.
31. Parham v. J.R., pp. 584-5.
32. Pavalon, *Human Rights and Health Care Law,* pp. 143-49.
33. Holder, *Legal Issues in Pediatrics and Adolescent Medicine,* pp. 147-8.

34. Ibid., p. 136; see also Memorial Hospital v. Maricopa County, 415 U.S. 250 (1974).
35. *Webster's New World Dictionary,* s.v. *diagnosis.*
36. Holder, *Medical Malpractice Law* (New York: John Wiley and Sons, 1975) p. 68.
37. Ibid., p. 65.
38. Ibid., p. 70; see also Evans, *A Practioner's Guide to Alcoholism and the Law,* p. 13.
39. *Quick Reference to Diagnostic Criteria DSM III* and the *DSM III* are available from Publication Sales, American Psychiatric Association, 1700 18th Street, N.W., Washington D.C. 20009.
40. John Mayer and William J. Filstead, "The Adolescent Alcohol Involvement Scale," *Journal of Studies on Alcohol,* Vol. 40, No. 3, 1979, p. 291.
41. Proceedings 2nd National DWI Conference, Rochester MN, AAA Foundation for Traffic Safety, 8111 Gatehouse Rd., Falls Church VA 22042 (1979).
42. To order MMPI tests, one source is Western Psychological Services, 12031 Wilshire Blvd., Los Angeles, CA 90025.
43. Proceedings, 2nd National DWI Conference, p. 43 has this list:
    1. Criteria Committee, National Council on Alcoholism. "Criteria for the diagnosis of alcoholism." *American Journal of Psychiatry,* 1972, pp. 127-135.
    2. Jacobson, G.R., "The Mortimer-Filkins Test: Court Procedures for Identifying Alcoholics." *Alcohol Health and Research World,* 1976 (Summer), pp. 22-26.
    3. Jacobson, G.R., *Diagnosis and Assessment of Alcohol Abuse and Alcoholism,* (Washington, D.C.: Alcohol, Drug Abuse, and Mental Health Administration, 1976) (DHEW Pub. No. ADM-76-228).
    4. Jacobson, G.R., *The Alcoholisms: Detection, Diagnosis, and Assessment,* (New York: Human Sciences Press, 1976).

5. Jacobson, G.R., Niles, D.H., Moberg, D.P., Mandehr, E., and Dusso, L. "Identifying Alcoholic and Problem-Drinking Drivers: Wisconsin's Field Test of a Modified NCA Criteria for the Diagnosis of Alcoholism." In Galanter, M. (Ed.) *Currents in Alcoholism, VI: Treatment, Rehabilitation, and Epidemeology.* (New York: Grune & Stratton, 1979).

6. Jacobson, G.R., and Lindsay, D. "Screening for Alcohol Problems among the Unemployed." In Galanter, M. (Ed.) *Currents in Alcoholism VIII: Treatment, Rehabilitation, and Epidemeology.* (New York: Grune & Stratton, 1980) (in press).

7. Selzer, M.L., "The Michigan Alcoholism Screening Test: The Quest for a New Diagnostic Instrument," *American Journal of Psychiatry,* Vol. 127, 1971, pp. 89-94.

Also contact the library at the Rutgers Center for Alcohol Studies, Smithers Hall, New Brunswick, NJ 08903, (201) 932- 2190.

44. For a list of all these laws see *The Mentally Disabled and the Law,* American Bar Association Foundation, 1971, Table 3.8, pp. 103-9.

45. H. Rutherford Turnbull III, ed., *Consent Handbook,* (Washington D.C.: American Association on Mental Deficiency 1977) p. 49.

46. Holder, *Medical Malpractice Law,* pp. 90-92.

47. Steven H. Gifis, *Law Dictionary,* (Woodbury, NY: Barrons Educational Series, Inc., 1975) p. 55.

48. Ibid., p. 119.

49. Ibid., p. 119.

50. Ibid., p. 195.

51. Inge N. Dobelis, ed., *Reader's Digest Family Legal Guide,* (Pleasantville, NY: 1981) p. 627.

52. Ibid., pp. 630-31.

53. Benjamin M. Schutz, *Legal Liability in Psychotherapy* (San Francisco, CA: Jossey-Bass Publishers, 1982) p. 11; see also Berry v. Moensch, 331 P 2d 814 (1958).

54. Dobelis, *Reader's Digest Family Legal Guide,* p. 631.
55. Ibid.
56. Ibid., p. 630.
57. Schutz, *Legal Liability in Psychotherapy,* pp. 10-11.
58. Ibid., pp. 53-78.
59. Ibid., p. 54.
60. Ibid., p. 5; Tarasoff v. Regents of the University of California, 529 P 2d 553 (1974), 551 P 2d 334 (1976); and see also McIntosh v. Milano, 168 N.J.S. 466 (1979); and Shaw v. Glickman, No. 1210, (MD App. 1980).
61. Shaw v. Glickman, No. 1210 (MD App. 1980).
62. Schutz, *Legal Liability in Psychotherapy,* p. 67.
63. Ibid.
64. Ibid., pp. 68-69.
65. Ibid., p. 74.
66. Ibid., pp. 74-5.
67. Available from Hazelden Educational Materials, order no. 1947.

VI
CONFIDENTIALITY

The law clearly favors the treatment of children. But at what point can, or must, the parents be told about treatment? What if a child refuses treatment for fear that parents or school officials will find out? What rights do parents have to be informed? Can a child disappear into a residential treatment program while the parents frantically call the police and fear the worst? Suppose a child has an alcoholic parent and needs treatment to deal with the parental problem? Should the parent be notified? If a student has an alcohol or other drug problem and discusses it with a high school guidance counselor, must the parents always be informed? The answer to these questions may vary from state to state; however, we can look at some guidelines that apply, including the Federal Alcohol and Drug Confidentiality Regulations,[1] the Pediatric Bill of Rights,[2] state law, and the Family Educational Rights and Privacy Act.[3] First, let's look at the Federal Alcohol and Drug Confidentiality Regulations.

The Federal Alcohol and Drug Confidentiality Regulations

These regulations cover all programs or individuals who furnish diagnosis, treatment, or referral for alcohol or other drug abuse and who received financial assistance from the federal government, or have an IRS tax exempt nonprofit status.[4] Most alcohol and other drug programs are covered by the regulations because they receive federal funds, or are nonprofit organizations. Even if your program is not covered by the regulations, if you receive information from a program that is covered, you have to protect the information as if you were covered.[5]

The regulations provide that in a state where a minor, without parental consent, can obtain alcohol or other drug treatment, diagnosis, counseling, or referral, any information on such a patient can only be released with the patient's special written consent, even if the patient is a minor. The minor, under state law, is now an adult for treatment purposes. The special written consent has ten parts, all of which must be filled out as required for it to be valid. (See the model form at the end of the book.) In addition, whenever any information is sent out in response to this consent, it must be accompanied by a specific statement prohibiting redisclosure unless it is in accordance with the regulations.[6]

If a minor is considered an adult for treatment purposes, the regulations do not even allow the treatment program to contact the parents to obtain payment for services, unless special written consent is obtained from the minor. If payment is required, and the minor cannot pay, treatment can be refused if the minor will not consent to contact the parents. However, if the program is legally bound to provide treatment irrespective of ability to pay, the minor should be admitted, and the parents cannot be given treatment information unless the minor provides written consent.[7]

If the minor lacks the capacity to make a rational decision whether to consent to notify his or her parents and the patient's condition poses a threat to his or her well-being or life, and such threat can be reduced by contacting the parents, the program may do so.[8]

If the minor cannot consent to treatment under state law, then the parents *and* the minor must sign the special written consent before there is any release of information; therefore, the minor still exercises some control over confidentiality.[9]

In those states where minors have adult treatment rights, an initial contact by a minor for treatment is protected. For example, if a minor calls a program and applies for services, but is turned down because payment is required, or for another reason, the contact is nevertheless confidential.[10]

Any information on a patient, verbal or written, on a medical record or elsewhere, that is created or acquired in connection with any alcohol or other drug abuse diagnosis, treatment, or referral for treatment, is covered by the Federal Confidentiality Regulations.[11] Also, anyone receiving such information from a program covered by the regulations cannot disclose it unless it is in accordance with the regulations.[12]

A patient can revoke the consent to release at any time. The one exception to this general rule is when a patient has been involved with the criminal justice system and has been sent to treatment instead of being confined. In this case, the patient cannot revoke consent until the criminal justice involvement is concluded.[13]

The above confidentiality protections may apply even if the child confesses a crime to the counselor, such as use or sale of drugs. Normally a counselor will not get into trouble by keeping this confidential.[14]

Without specific written consent, a program cannot release information except for medical emergencies, research, or audit purposes, or in response to a special court order.[15] A medical emergency is any situation that threatens the life or health of a patient. In order to deal with the emergency, you can release information to medical personnel, i.e., emergency room personnel, physicians, etc. You may need to utilize this in drug overdose cases, suicide attempts, child abuse, or other medical emergencies.[16]

A situation where you can release information without consent is in response to a special court order. This is a unique type of court order made only after a hearing, to which the treatment program must receive notice and has the right to be represented by counsel. The patient must also receive notice and has the right to counsel. These orders can only be issued for good cause, i.e., where the social interest in the release of information is more important than the confidentiality, or to investigate a crime which involves or threatens loss of life or bodily injury, such as child abuse.[17]

Subpoenas and Search Warrants

A subpoena or search warrant alone is not a special court order under the regulations. The regulations require that before a subpoena or search warrant is proper, a special court hearing as described above must take place.[18]

If a program receives a subpoena without this special hearing first taking place, the program should contact the court or person who issued the subpoena and inform them of the regulations *and* the fact that they need a special court order. Information cannot be provided without it. If the lawyer or court who issues the subpoena insists the program come to court anyway, the program should go to court in response to the subpoena and inform the judge of the regulations making it clear it is illegal to testify without the hearing. The program's attorney should be there. The patient, who is the subject of the subpoena, also has a right to an attorney. If the judge orders the program to testify, it may have no choice. Let the program's attorney handle it after that.

If the police come to the program's door with a search warrant and they insist on coming in, even after being informed regarding the regulations and the need for a special court order, let them in, but contact your program's attorney so he or she can immediately go to court to correct the situation.

Pediatric Bill of Rights

In addition to the Federal Regulations, another authority concerned with minors' confidentiality is the Pediatric Bill of Rights of the National Association of Children's Hospitals. It states a minor's treatment must be kept confidential in accordance with the normal rules of a treater-patient relationship if consent from a parent is not required at the time the relationship begins.[19] Although it does not have the force of law, it is a good professional guideline.

State Laws

In most states, if the program is not governed by the federal regulations, it will have to abide by the state's confidentiality or *privilege* laws. Many states extend confidentiality protection to physicians, nurses, and other medical personnel, psychologists, social workers, marriage counselors, clergy, attorneys, and drug counselors.[20] Check your state law.

Although confidentiality is granted under state law, there may be some exceptions. For example, in medical emergencies or potential suicides where information must be released to save the patient's life and the patient cannot or will not give consent, where there is an infectious disease or child abuse, or when a patient threatens another and a warning is necessary to protect the intended victim, or where there is a criminal investigation.[21]

Parental Alcohol or Other Drug Problems

If a child has an alcoholic or drug abusing parent and seeks counseling, must parents be notified? When the laws were written giving children the right to treatment, they were intended to help children get treatment for their own problems, not those of others. However, many of the laws are written in a way that can be interpreted to allow treatment of a child of an alcoholic or other drug addict even if the child isn't an alcoholic or other drug abuser. Such laws should be interpreted to the child's benefit. In those states with no minor's right to treatment laws, treatment may still be rendered under the mature minor rule or some other legal device. If treatment can be given to the child, confidentiality will apply and parents don't have to be told. Of course, treatment should be aimed at getting the total family involved.

Child Abuse

If the child you are treating is a victim of child abuse, you may have to report it depending on your state law. Most states require such reporting, even if there is a physician-patient privilege. Under the Federal Alcohol and Drug Regulations you can report it, if your patient is the victim, as long as you do not reveal confidential treatment information about the patient. By reporting abuse you are revealing information about the abuser and not your patient. What if the abuser is your patient? Suppose the whole family is in treatment, or just one of the parents, when you find out about child abuse? The Federal Regulations do not require you to report abuse, even if there is a state law that says you must.[22] However, you can still report the abuse in any of these ways: (1) You can report it anonymously to the police or a child protection agency, i.e., you don't reveal your professional involvement with the patient, but you state who is doing the abusing and where they live. The child protection agency should respond to anonymous information. (2) You can seek a court order under Subpart E of the Federal Regulations. (3) You can report it to medical personnel if there is a *bona fide* medical emergency.[23] (4) You can get patient consent to report it. (5) You can report it via a *qualified service organization agreement,* which is a written agreement between the treatment program and the police or child protection agency.[24] In such an agreement, the child protection agency would have to maintain confidentiality in accordance with the Federal Regulations while enabling the treatment program to comply with both the Federal Regulations and the state child abuse reporting laws.

Under this agreement, the child protection agency would be a qualified service organization and be bound by the Federal

Regulations in handling patient information from the program.
Under the agreement, the child protection agency would agree
to provide services aimed at preventing or treating child
abuse, such as day-care, counseling, and other such services
to patients suspected of child abuse. In order to meet the
requirements of the Federal Regulations, the child protection
agency would, in the written agreement,

1) acknowledge that it is bound by the Federal Regulations
   in the handling of any alcohol or other drug abuse
   patient information received from the treatment provider;

2) agree to implement appropriate procedures for safe-
   guarding the information; and

3) agree to resist, in judicial proceedings, any efforts to
   obtain access to patient information except as expressly
   provided in the Federal Regulations.[25]

If a child protection agency wants to use the information
obtained under the qualified services organization agreement
for the purpose of criminal prosecution of the abuser, it must
obtain an authorizing court order in accordance with the
regulations.

Parents' Rights to Treatment Information

In general, under the law, if a minor can enter treatment
without parental consent, a program must be careful in
releasing confidential treatment information to parents. Does
this mean parents cannot learn the whereabouts of their
children? Not necessarily. Programs could require that parents
be notified as part of acceptance into treatment. Such programs could refuse to provide treatment without parental
consent, even if the law allows the child to be treated without
it. The only exception to this might be a publicly supported
program set up to treat children for free. Usually, however,

the child will consent to informing his or her parents, especially if payment is required, or if the child knows the parents cannot take him or her out of treatment. Another way to inform parents is for the program to notify a child protection agency of the child's safety, and the agency could notify the parents without revealing the treatment situation of the child. In order to do this, the program may want to consider creating a qualified service organization agreement in which the child protection agency agrees to protect the child's confidentiality.

In the meantime, or instead of the above, if the program thought it was useful to have the parents obtain information, the program could seek a court order allowing the parents to obtain more information. If the parents discover by their own efforts where the child is, they can seek a court order also. In addition, some authorities assert that you could notify the parents of the child's location, but not that the child is in treatment.

If a treatment program makes a mistake, either by informing the parents or not, the risk of being sued is very low. The best procedure is to check the law, decide what is best for the child, and then make the decision.

If a child does not have the right to treatment, then the parents should be informed, and they have the right with the child to control which information is to be released to other parties.[26]

Schools and Confidentiality

Normally, school officials and teachers are not bound by treatment confidentiality laws. However, there may be state laws that specifically deal with school drug programs. In any case, federal laws may apply, especially if your school sets up a SAP.

Schools and the Federal Alcohol and Drug Confidentiality Regulations

Whether a minor student has the right to consent to treatment or not, a SAP would first have to determine whether it was bound by the Federal Alcohol and Drug Confidentiality Regulations. If the school program receives federal financial assistance for an alcohol or other drug abuse identification, referral, or treatment function, the records of the program may be covered by the regulations.[27] If this is the case, information about the student's treatment cannot be released except as discussed earlier. It requires a special type of written consent form, as described in the regulations, to be signed by the student and maybe the parents.[28] Information could also be released for a medical emergency, program audit, or special court order. If the school uses an outside agency for identification, referral, and treatment of students, and if that agency is covered by the regulations, they cannot give information back to the school, nor can they release the information to anyone else, unless the special consent form is signed. If the school receives the information after such written consent is given, the school must treat it as confidential in accordance with the regulations, even if the school is not covered by the regulations.[29]

Family Educational Rights and Privacy Act

If the school program is not covered by the Federal Alcohol and Drug Confidentiality Regulations and it is a public school or otherwise receives federal education funds, it will have to abide by the requirements of the Family Educational Rights and Privacy Act of 1974.[30] This federal law gives parents the right to inspect and review all educational records directly relating to their children (under eighteen) which are maintained by an educational agency or institution, or party acting for the agency or institution.[31] Educational records can include SAP records. Such records, however, do *not* include such things as private records of teachers or other school personnel, records of law enforcement units in a school, and employment records of school personnel.[32] Parents have no right to review these records. As a result, some teachers or

SAP personnel label their counseling notes as their own private records, thus keeping them confidential from parents. Parents also cannot review records of students eighteen or older, or records of children attending a post-secondary educational institution, which are "created by or maintained by a physician, psychiatrist, psychologist, or other recognized professional or paraprofessional capacity or assisting in that capacity" and which were "created, maintained, or used only in connection with the provision of treatment to the student," and which were "not disclosed to anyone other than individuals providing treatment; provided that the records can be personally reviewed by a physician or other appropriate professional of the student's choice."[33]

This means students eighteen years or older who are treated by a school treatment professional have confidentiality protection and the school must get their written consent before releasing information. If the student is under eighteen, the law implies parents can review such treatment records.

If the school is covered only by the Family Educational Rights and Privacy Act, the school must let parents see the records and cannot release educational records of a student under eighteen without the parents' consent. If the student is over eighteen or in college, the school must get the student's consent in place of the parents' consent.[34]

Parents have the right to request correction of any incorrect information in the student's records. Students over eighteen or in college also have this right. This right can be exercised informally or by having a hearing in which the parents or student can correct the information.[35]

In the case of a medical or safety emergency, the Act allows information to be released without consent if the emergency is serious, the information is necessary to meet it, and it is given out on a need to know.[36]

Parents and school officials, as well as SAP programs, should become familiar with this Act. Contact the school principal or administrator for details. They are required by the law to provide information on the Act.[37]

Conflict of Laws

If the school's SAP program is covered by the Federal Alcohol and Drug Confidentiality Regulations and a minor under eighteen has the right to treatment under state law with adult treatment confidentiality rights, there may be a conflict between the Alcohol and Drug Regulations, the state law, and the Family Educational Rights and Privacy Act all three of which may apply to the school. In such cases, seek a legal opinion on how the state law applies to the federal laws.[38]

Chapter 6
ENDNOTES

1. 42 CFR, Part 2. As of April, 1985, these Regulations are being revised. Proposed revision published in Federal Register, Vol. 48, no. 166, August 25, 1983, p. 38758. Further revisions will be published in the Federal Register. Compliance with state child abuse reporting laws may be required under the new revisions. Check to see what final revisions are.
2. Angela Roddey Holder, LL.M., *Legal Issues in Pediatrics and Adolescent Medicine,* (New York: John Wiley and Sons, 1977) p. 155; see also G. Emmett Rait, Jr., "The Minor's Right to Consent to Medical Treatment", 48 *So. Cal. Law Rev.,* p. 1417 (1975).
3. 20 U.S.C. 1232 (g); Title 45 Public Welfare Subtitle A, DHHS, Part 99, sec. 99.5.
4. 42 CFR, Part 2, sec. 2.12.
5. Ibid. sec. 2.32.
6. David G. Evans, *A Practitioner's Guide to Alcoholism and the Law,* (Center City, MN: Hazelden, 1983) pp. 21-28; see 42 CFR, Part 2, sec. 2.15, 2.31, 2.32.
7. Ibid., sec. 2.15.
8. Ibid.
9. Ibid.
10. Ibid.

11. Ibid., sec. 2.11.
12. 42 CFR, Part 2, sec. 2.32.
13. 42 CFR, Part 2, sec. 2.39.
14. 42 CFR, Part 2, sec. 2.23.
15. 42 CFR, Part 2, Subpart D and E.
16. 42 CFR, Part 2, Subpart D, sec. 2.51.
17. 42 CFR, Part 2, Subpart E; and see Federal Register Vol. 48., no. 166, August 25, 1983, Subpart E, sec. 2.64.
18. 42 CFR, Part 2, Subpart E.
19. See endnote 2 above.
20. Hammonds v. Aetna, 243 F. Supp. 793 (N.D. Ohio, 1965); see also American Medical Association, Principles of Medical Ethics, sec. 9 (1957); see also American Medical Association, Judicial Council Opinions and Reports, sec. 5.62 (1977); Horne v. Patton, 287 So. 2d 824 (Ala. 1973); New Jersey Rules of Evidence, Privileges (Newark, N.J.: Gann Law Books); Emanual Hayt, LL.B., *Medicolegal Aspects of Hospital Records,* (Berwyn: IL, Physician's Record Company, 1977); see 71 Penn. Stat. sec. 1690.108 for a strict state confidentiality law for alcohol and drug treatment.
21. Holder, *Legal Issues in Pediatrics and Adolescent Medicine,* p. 155; Evans, *A Practitioner's Guide to Alcoholism and the Law,* pp. 21-28.
22. 42 CFR, Part 2, sec. 2.32; and see Federal Child Abuse and Treatment Act 42 U.S.C. 101; and State v. Andring, 342 N.W. 2d 123 (1984); be sure to check the revised Regulations on this point, endnote 1 above.
23. 42 CFR, Part 2, sec. 2.51.
24. "Confidentiality of Alcohol and Drug Abuse Patient Records and Child Abuse and Neglect Reporting," *Alcohol, Health and Research World,* (Rockville, MD: NIAAA, 1979).
25. 42 CFR, Part 2, sec. 2.11.
26. 42 CFR, Part 2, sec. 2.15.
27. 42 CFR, Part 2, sec. 2.12.

28. 42 CFR, Part 2, sec. 2.31.
29. 42 CFR, Part 2, sec. 2.32.
30. See endnote 3 above.
31. Ibid.
32. Title 45 Public Welfare, Subtitle A, DHHS, Part 99, sec. 99.3.
33. Ibid.
34. Ibid., sec. 99.4.
35. Ibid., sec. 99.20 and 21.
36. Ibid., sec. 99.36.
37. Ibid., sec. 99.5.
38. Ibid., sec. 99.61; and see opinion letter no. 79-23, dated June 27, 1979, from the Office of the General Counsel, HHS, to Ms. Patricia A. Mulready regarding conflict between Federal Alcohol and Drug Confidentiality Regulations and the Family Educational Rights and Privacy Act. The opinion letter is available from the Department of Health and Human Services.

VII
CHILDREN OF ALCOHOLICS AND OTHER DRUG ADDICTS, AND CHILD ADVOCACY

I could not write this book without talking about the rights of children whose parents are addicted to alcohol or other drugs. Much more needs to be done to help these children who are so often abused or neglected. The law has moved slowly to help them, but the law only reflects the attitudes of society.

These children need legal and other forms of advocacy to help them get through legal, and bureaucratic barriers.[1] Being an advocate for such a child doesn't require legal or social work training. The involvement of professionals is desirable, but not always necessary. Self-help groups and victim advocacy groups can do wonders in cutting through red tape or helping enact legal reforms. If you have a group in your area that helps children of alcoholics or other drug abusers, urge them to consider a child advocacy program or start your own. You can also do a lot of good on an individual level.

Remember, the use of legal procedures to get help for children or their parents should only be tried after attempts at counseling or persuasion have failed. You always risk that the legal system may not respond properly because of ignorance about the nature of alcohol and other drug problems. If there is no other way to help a child, do what you must.

By helping these children, we help their children and their grandchildren. Many drug addicts had parents who were also ill with addictive problems.

The three general kinds of laws that can help these children

Kids, Drugs, and the Law

are those concerned with abuse and neglect, family court, and
involuntary commitment for adults.

Abuse and Neglect

Abuse is a nonaccidental mental or physical injury, or a
sexual molestation.[2] Sometimes parents and others feel they
have the right to beat a child or take other measures to
"guide" or "discipline" a child. It is true that parents can
establish reasonable rules for their children's conduct, and
they have the right to administer punishment or restraint of
the child.[3] However, parents cannot inflict punishment which
is excessive, immoderate, or unreasonable.[4] Punishments such
as beatings resulting in injury, head-shaving, chaining, tying
up, or locking up a child have been found to be excessive.[5]
Neglect may be failure to provide proper support, education,
medical or other care, abandonment, or subjecting a child to
an injurious environment.[6]

Depending on state law, various health and educational
personnel are required to report abuse or neglect to a state
child protection agency or to the police. Over twenty states
mandate that any citizen with knowledge of abuse or neglect
must report it.[7] People who report such abuse should not fear
they can be sued for libel, slander, or invasion of privacy, as
all states provide immunity from liability for a good-faith
reporting by citizens, institutions, or agencies.[8]

If a state child protection agency, in response to a report,
conducts an investigation and confirms the abuse, they will
get involved with the family. This involvement will range in
seriousness from a request to obtain voluntary counseling to
the filing of criminal charges. Some states even allow law
enforcement officials, health officials, and child protection
agencies to summarily take protective custody of a child.[9]

The problem with using these laws is that often the state
child abuse protection agency or other officials are not
properly trained in how to detect and treat chemical

dependency problems. Very often the parents are not even asked to be evaluated for such problems, and as a result the main cause of the problem remains unchecked. Proper child advocacy in these situations can ensure the addictive problems of the parents are addressed.

Family Court or Juvenile Court

Utilizing your state family court or juvenile court is another useful tool in helping children. Depending on local law, the court may be able to provide assistance even in those cases that do not involve serious abuse or neglect.[10] Such cases involve situations where the home environment is not healthy and the child's emotional development is being negatively affected, but the basic necessities for the child are present. For example, one state law provides for situations where a parent abuses lawful parental authority or where there are problems in the family that cause the child to be truant or act out in other ways. This same law requires that if "as a result of any information supplied on the family situation" where the court personnel have "reason to believe that the parent or guardian is an alcoholic. . .or a drug dependent person," the court personnel "shall state the basis for this determination and provide recommendations to the court."[11] As a result, the court can order the parents into treatment. This law also requires that court personnel who handle these matters must receive "training in drug and alcohol abuse."

The child abuse and neglect laws and the family court laws have a wide range of options available. A well-informed child advocate can press the court to use those options that will provide for drug evaluations and treatment. It is important in trying to help a child that you get the court to have the parents evaluated by an experienced chemical dependency professional; otherwise, the parents may talk the court out of

Kids, Drugs, and the Law

it. If the evaluation indicates there is a problem, ask the court to order treatment. Go to bat for the children! Who else is going to?

Removing the Child from the Home

The courts usually do not like to terminate all of a parent's rights and remove the child from the home. Usually a court will only do this upon "clear and convincing" evidence it will be in the best interests of the child.[12] It may not be realistic to ask a court to remove a child unless there is real physical danger to the child. If the court will order the parent or parents into treatment instead, there may be no reason to remove the child.

Commitment Laws

If one of the parents or other family members are willing, they may be able to go into court to obtain an involuntary commitment for an addicted parent. Check your state law to see whether alcoholics and other drug abusers can be committed.[13] A commitment may be hard to get because it may require a physician's or other mental health professional's affidavit.

All of the methods mentioned for getting parents into treatment are not as useful as getting parents to go of their own free will. If you cannot talk the parents into it, seek professional counseling to help you. If that doesn't work, get a lawyer and other help to use the legal system. Some states will appoint a *guardian ad litem* for a child to help in family matters.[14]

Remember, if you wish to be a child advocate, you are on the side of both the child *and* the parents. Advocates need to be positive, helpful, well-informed, and *firm*. Everybody wants to do the right thing, and sometimes the child advocate just helps them do it.

If you are going to use the law to help a child, *be prepared.* Expect that the facts you present may be denied, contested, or twisted. Get your facts together, be honest, and in the words of Winston Churchill, "Never give up, never, never, never give up."

Chapter 7
ENDNOTES

1. Tom Christoffel, *Health and the Law, A Handbook for Health Professionals* (New York: The Free Press, 1982) p. 422; Claudia Black, *My Dad Loves Me, My Dad Has a Disease. A Workbook for Children of Alcoholics,* (Newport, CA: ACT); Booz, Allen and Hamilton Inc, *An Assessment of the Needs of and Resources for Children of Alcoholic Parents,* (Rockville, MD: NIAAA, 1979); see also the Hazelden catalog for materials on this subject. For a free catalog call toll free: (800) 328-9000.
2. Christoffel, *Health and the Law, a Handbook for Health Professionals,* p. 46; and see generally, The New York Family Court Act.
3. Arnold O. Ginnow and George Gordon, eds. *Corpus juris Secundum,* (St. Paul, MN: West Publishing Co.) 67A, Parent and Child, sec. 12.
4. Ibid.
5. Inge N. Dobelis, ed., *Readers Digest Family Legal Guide,* (Pleasantville, N.Y., 1981) p. 565; see also State v. Black, 227 S.W. 2d 1006; Hinkle v. State, 46 Ind 777; Roe v. Conn., 417 F. Supp. 769.
6. Christoffel, *Health and the Law, a Handbook for Health Professionals,* p. 416.
7. Ibid., p. 416.
8. Ibid., p. 41.
9. Ibid., p. 419.
10. Delaware Code Title 10, Chapter 9, sec. 921.

11. N.J.S. 2 A: 4A-83; N.J.S. 2A:4A 22(g); N.J. Court Rule 5:15-1 and 5:15-2; N.J.S. 26: 2B-8; N.J.S. 24: 21-2.
12. "Child Abuse," *American Bar Association Journal,* (August 1983) p. 1009; Santosky v. Kramer, 455 US 745.
13. Connecticut General Statute 17-155Y (c) and 19-498; Allan Luks, ed., "Forced Treatment Grows" *Legal Issues,* International Council on Alcohol and Addiction, (March 1982) 133 East 62nd St., New York, NY 10021; see also Vernon's Annotated Texas Civil Statutes Act 5561c (9-18); Cameron v. Mullin, 387 F 2d 193 (D.C. Cir. 1967); People v. Lally, 224 N.E. 2d 87, 277; Bolton v. Harris, 395 F 2d 642 (D.C. Cir. 1968); N.C. Gen. Stat., sec. 58:22 and 23, also 122-58.7 (1981); Cal. Welf. Institutions Code, sec. 5172, 3050, and 3200; DC Code Ann. Sec. 24-527 and 24-603-8; MD. H.G. Gen. 8-506 and 9-620; NJSA 30:9-12:21; see also endnote 29 in Chapter 6 on Treatment.
14. "Lawyers for Kids," *American Bar Association Journal,* (August 1983) p. 11011; see also NJSA 3A: 6- 16(10); and NJSA 3A:6-36.

CLOSING

I hope this book has both answered and raised questions, and you have found it helpful. My intent was to acquaint you with the legal tools to help kids with alcohol and other drug problems. I want you to understand that, although the law needs improvement, it is on your side and you can use it. In the future, I hope you and I can point with pride to the changes we have made. Let's get to work!

To those young people and parents who need to recover, here is a favorite passage from the book *Alcoholics Anonymous:**

> Abandon yourself to God as you understand God.
> Admit your faults to Him and to your fellows. Clear
> away the wreckage of your past. Give freely of what
> you find and join us. We shall be with you in the
> Fellowship of the Spirit, and you will surely meet
> some of us as you trudge the Road of Happy Destiny.,
> May God bless you and keep you — until then.

---

*Alcoholics Anonymous, (New York: Alcoholics Anonymous World Services, Inc., 1976).

HOW TO FIND A LAW

The endnotes for this book contain *cites* to various laws
and court cases. Citing is a system which uses numbers and
subject headings to locate laws in books or on computers.

Statutes are cited by a numerical code and a subject heading. For example, the New Jersey intoxicated driving law is
cited as New Jersey Statutes Annotated (NJSA) 39:4-50 (the
numerical code), "Operation of Motor Vehicles by Persons
under the Influence of Liquor or Drugs" (the subject heading). If we wanted to find this law we would look in the New
Jersey Statutes Annotated for the numerical code or in the
statutes' index for topics that would lead us to the subject of
intoxicated driving. For example, under *intoxication* there
would be a subtopic on "Motor Vehicle Operation While
Intoxicated."

Administrative law uses the same type of citing system as
statutory law. For example, the Federal Confidentiality Regulations from the Department of Health and Human Services are
cited as "Confidentiality of Alcohol and Drug Abuse Patient
Records" (subject heading), "42 CFR (Code of Federal
Regulations), Part 2" (numerical code). This law is found in
volume 42 of the CFR in Part 2.

Court law is cited differently. Each court with the power to
make law will write an opinion in a case so others can read
what the law is. These opinions are published in books called
reporters. The citation for a court case will give the name of
the case (the plaintiff versus defendant) and the volume and

page number of the reporter which contains the case. For example, such a case citation would read "Collins vs. Hand, 431 Pa. 378." Collins is the plaintiff, Hand is the defendant, and the case is found in Volume 431 of *The Pennsylvania Reporter* on page 378. *The Pennsylvania Reporter* is a state reporter. There are also regional reporters which contain the cases from a group of states, such as *The Pacific Reporter* (P) or *The Atlantic Reporter* (A). If the reporter is in its second series of publication, it will have a *2nd* after it. For example, the second series of the *Atlantic Reporter* is cited as *A 2nd*.

Laws and reporters are available in some public libraries, but it is better to go to a law library. The best law libraries are found in law schools or in state libraries. These libraries will have the laws and cases of your state, other states, and the federal government. Your county court house will also have a law library but it may only cover your state law and cases.

Lawyers and law librarians are trained in legal research. They can find laws and cases with little information to go on. However, if you want to find a law or get a legal opinion, it is best to give them a cite. The cites in this book will be very helpful to them in locating the law which pertains to your case. Please use them.

CONSENT FORM*

1. I (name of patient)   Request   Authorize

2. (Program which is to make the disclosure)

3. To disclose: (kind and amount of information to be disclosed)

4. To: (name or title of the person or organization to which disclosure is to be made)

5. For: (purpose of the disclosure)

6. Date:

7. Signature of patient

8. Signature of parent or guardian (where required)

9. Signature of person authorized to sign in lieu of patient (where required)

10. This consent is subject to revocation at any time except to the extent that the program which is to make the disclosure has already taken action in reliance on it. If not previously revoked, this consent will terminate upon: (specific date, event, or condition).

---

*Source — Federal Register, Vol. 48, No. 166, August 25, 1983. Sec. 2.31 — see also 2.32 for statement on prohibition on redisclosure, which is different from the one found in 42 CFR Part 2, as of April, 1985. See endnote 1 in Chapter 6 on Confidentiality.